"If a pilgrimage to Friuli was not already on your bucket list, there's no doubt it should be now. Bobby Stuckey and Lachlan Mackinnon-Patterson's restaurant Frasca is a mandatory stop for food and wine lovers everywhere. And now with *Friuli Food and Wine*, the two have taken us along on an entertaining and scholarly journey to the inspirational roots of the restaurant, capturing the essence and magic of Friuli Venezia Giulia—its wine, its food, and its welcoming hospitality."

DANNY MEYER, founder and CEO of Union Square Hospitality Group

"I first discovered Frasca, my favourite restaurant in America, in 2008 whilst on tour with Rush . . . and so began an education and love affair with an underappreciated corner of Italy called Friuli Venezia Giulia. This exquisitely produced and passionately written book is a must-have for all lovers of good food and wine. Bobby, Lachlan, and Meredith, along with the Frasca team, have brought Friuli to life through these recipes."

GEDDY LEE, bassist and vocalist of Rush

Friuli
FOOD AND WINE

Frasca Cooking from Northern Italy's
Mountains, Vineyards, and Seaside

Bobby Stuckey,
Lachlan Mackinnon-Patterson,
and Meredith Erickson

Photographs by William Hereford

TEN SPEED PRESS
California | New York

61 Land

129 Sea

191 Mountains

Carnic Alps

INTRODUCTION

by Bobby Stuckey

Friuli is where we truly learned about hospitality. The entire region and its people seem to breathe it. Let me give you an example.

In 2014, our good friend and restaurant peer Sam Beall, owner of Blackberry Farm in Tennessee (one of the greatest hospitality destinations and hotels in the world), asked us to take twenty guests on a cycling trip to Friuli Venezia Giulia (FVG, or simply "Friuli") in the northeastern corner of Italy. We stayed at La Subida (see page 94), an inn run by the Sirk family (Jŏsko, Loredana, and their children, Tanja and Mitja) that had become our home away from home in Friuli after many years of visiting the area.

On the final day, we opted to cycle to the top of Monte Zoncolan, one of the longest and most classic climbs in the Carnic Alps and a 130-kilometer cycle from La Subida. Ninety-five kilometers into the ride, we had just reached the foot of Zoncolan when we noticed Jŏsko coming up on his motorcycle! He had ridden out to see us off on our climb, which was a huge gesture because the family was hosting a wedding at the hotel that day. Some three kilometers later, while traversing what is one of the steepest paved roads in Italy, we spotted him again—a moment of heartwarming relief from the deep physical pain.

The very last part of the climb is an eight-kilometer stretch that took most of us more than an hour to complete. Passing through a final tunnel to the summit, who should be waiting on the other side? None other than Jŏsko, who greeted us with magnums of Bjana sparkling wine. He sabered the bottles and waited more than an hour for all of the riders to finish, handing each a glass and a piece of home-baked strudel. As soon as the final rider had pulled up, Jŏsko motored back to the restaurant and worked the wedding.

The Sirk family will make you an espresso when it's still dark outside, scoop fresh yogurt made on the next hillside for your breakfast, or offer bottles of sparkling wine at the end of a long climb. That's hospitality. And that's Friuli.

In 2003, Lachlan and I moved to the culinary middle-of-nowhere in Colorado to open a restaurant where the food and wine would be inspired by the relative middle-of-nowhere Friuli Venezia Giulia, Italy. We had both just finished working at the French Laundry in Napa Valley and were looking for a fresh start and complete change from everything we had known. Boulder offered the mountains for cycling and running, but also physical space and head space. Our good friend (and a winemaker) Raj Parr tried to stage an intervention to stop us (along with my wife, Danette) from moving to this charming but frankly somewhat provincial town to open our own place—all to no avail.

The year before our move, we visited FVG with Nate Ready, our opening sommelier. At that point, we had already been seduced by, and were forcefully experimenting with, the wines of Friuli—from producers such as Radikon and Gravner—that are in fashion now but back then were edge-of-the-world-type stuff. The four of us had gotten on a plane to Venice and traveled an hour northeast to the border of Italy and Slovenia for what turned out to be the first of many pilgrimages. And although we had already built up the region in our minds, it exceeded expectations on every level. Nothing intrigued us more than the people, wine, and food of Friuli Venezia Giulia.

FVG is the southernmost piece of what was the Austrian Empire in the early 1800s and, for a brief moment, the Austro-Hungarian Empire in the late 1800s. It also contains a piece of Slavic culture to the west, all of which collide at the port city of Trieste, one of the only major ports of the former Austrian Empire. Access to Trieste brought Austrians everything from spices to coffee beans, and infused Friulano cuisine with elements of many cultures as shipments made their way along the road from the port to Vienna. Trieste was one of the first polyglot cities, combining Jewish and Eastern European cultural traditions in Western Europe. Italians consider FVG to be more Austrian or Slavic than Italian. And the administrative region of Friuli Venezia Giulia as we know it today was not wholly formed and didn't belong to Italy until 1954. Before that date, Friuli was part-Italian, part-Slovenian, and part-Croatian. In fact, Friuli was once considered the western region of the area that included the eastern region of Venezia Giulia, which was connected to the Adriatic; hence the combined name.

The cuisine of Friuli paints a beautiful picture of this fragmented history. No other part of Italy (with the exception, perhaps, of Sicily) has been influenced by so many cultures and cuisines. FVG has been occupied by the Slavs, the Ottomans, the Venetians, the Austrians, the French (Napoleon brought French grapes to the area), and the Romans (the area was named after Julius Caesar). It's a little less sunny than Tuscany and a little more mysterious too. This is a place that balances on the fringe of east and west . . . where the food and people are simple yet sophisticated, and the wine is esoteric yet incredibly versatile. This tiny sliver of land is home to one of the most refined food and wine cultures in the world, and yet it remains relatively unknown.

Literary Friuli

Friuli is a land of castles and giants and princes, rich for both fiction and reality as the history books tell us. After World War I, Ernest Hemingway spent a lot of time in Friuli and it was here that he wrote *A Farewell to Arms*. For a decade, James Joyce lived in Trieste, where he raised his family and wrote *A Portrait of the Artist as a Young Man* and parts of *Ulysses*. The great Pier Paolo Pasolini's mother was from Friuli; he famously wrote his earliest poems and scripts in Friulian dialect and considered it his true home.

Italy is divided into many different regions: some have the food, some have the wine, but very few have both. Take Bologna, for instance. While the food culture there has depth, you can only drink so much Lambrusco. And Tuscany, with its beautiful sunsets and the rich cultural center of Florence, has incredible Brunellos and Chianti, but the cuisine—*Bistecca alla Fiorentina* and all—is less high-wattage and diverse. Sure, you'll find the occasional pizzeria in Friuli. There *is* red sauce, of course. But that's not *the jam*.

During our first trip to Friuli, Lachlan said, "This is the best Italian food I never knew existed." Up until that point, he had mainly been cooking at French restaurants in Paris and the United States (like the French Laundry), and his experience with French provisions ran deep. But right away the cuisine of Friuli Venezia Giulia felt like our *thing*: not only through the prism of wine but also because the dishes felt both familiar and exotic. Tagliolini al Portonat (page 103) is a great example of this, it's a simple pasta sauced with cream and a hit of poppy seeds that's deeply infused and *wrapped in* San Daniele prosciutto. It's so easy, so delicious, and yet so unlike anything we had seen on American menus. Before we opened Frasca, we had never been to a restaurant in the States that served Toc' in Braide (page 75), a rich, creamy polenta cooked in a Parmesan broth that is perhaps the most famous recipe in Friuli. Though Lidia Bastianich has shined a light on Friuli's food and wine (having spent her early childhood in Trieste), the cuisine is still not widely known nor close to popular.

Coming from a place that seems so exotic and mysterious, Friulano cuisine is actually quite accessible and translates well to home pantries and kitchens. When we first visited, we were surprised to find the food to be incredibly straightforward but with little glimpses of unexpected flavors, like anise, dill, cinnamon, caraway, ginger, and smoky paprika, all of which highlight Friuli's history as a central market in the spice trade. We have always felt that with food and wine, the past gives you a good perspective on the future. This is helpful for relationships, and works with recipes and culture too. How wonderful is a simple potato gnocchi with the singular smell of smoked ricotta (from the Carnic Alps) and a garnish of poppy seeds that came through the port of Trieste? Three products, one each by way of land, mountain, and sea, all on a single, simple plate.

San Giorgio, Carnic Alps

Geography is really the key to understanding Friuli. It has midlands, with the cultural capital of Udine and the lush vineyards of the Collio Goriziano and Colli Orientali. It has the Adriatic Sea, with the lagoons of Grado and Aquileia, as well as the port city of Trieste. And it has the Carnic Alps, shouldering Austria to the north and nearly hiding the veiled mountain towns of Tarvisio, Sauris, and Tolmezzo. Specifically, the region of Friuli Venezia Giulia is made up of four provinces. Udine (the largest, occupies over half of Friuli, stretching from the Alps down to the Adriatic, its main city the namesake. The western region of Pordenone is all plains, and includes the Friuli Grave DOC (*Denominazione di Origine Controlla*, or Denomination of Origin), which rubs shoulders with the Veneto (and its capital city, Venice). Gorizia has all the best vineyards of the region, including the Collio; the Slovenia-leaning town of Oslavia; and the seaside towns of Aquileia, Grado, and Monfalcone. And then there's Trieste, which is made up of the port city and all of the neighboring roads and towns (including the wine region of the Carso) that lead to it, like a cliff-side red carpet. All of this is in a region the size of Delaware. A good part of the answer to the question of why the deliciousness of Friuli exists is simply due to the topography. The other key part lies with its people and its history.

In 1976, much of the region was decimated by an earthquake, and this seems to have set off the *rimboccare le maniche* (roll-up-the-sleeves) spirit that we have personally encountered in everyone we've met, from farmers and winemakers to chefs, designers, and mechanics. This is a proud, humble group of people who have mastered techniques to take *cucina povera* (peasant cooking) and elevate it to its most noble—all the while staying tied to their roots. The air of FVG, the land and its traditions, feel completely unique—as though this place will never change. One time, we had dinner with Michele Boem, former head of tourism for Friuli. In his Friulano accent, he said, "Bobby, you know two million Americans come to Italy every year. Thirty [of those] come to Friuli, and twenty of *those* are your guests and employees!" He might have been exaggerating, but we have been in Friuli with our staff for an entire week in the high-season month of July and only run into one other American, and that American was restaurateur Joe Bastianich. It's geographically so close to Venice, which has millions of visitors a year, but FVG couldn't be farther from it culturally.

———

The word *frasca* means "branch" or "bough" and refers to the Friulian tradition of hanging a branch outside a property as a sign that there is new wine to sell. The typical frasca was originally a small family farm or wine estate where paying guests were served a taste of homemade prosciutto and (usually) a glass of Tocai Friulano, often at an outdoor table set under something beautifully flowering or fruiting or budding. While we don't know the exact origin of the frasca, we have heard it goes back to the days of the *osmize*, a tradition deriving from the Slovenian word for "eight" and the period in 1784 during which Emperor Josef II gave farmers in the Carso (now part of Friuli) eight days to sell their surplus goods directly from their homes. *Frasche* (the plural form of *frasca*) of this kind still flourish—in the spring, when the previous year's white wines

Lachlan (left) and Bobby (right) in the Collio

Ovaro, Carnic Alps

are ready, and in late fall, when the same vintage's reds are opened—but many frasche have evolved into what are now called *agriturismi* (farm stays). Although time has passed, we can confirm that the region is still dotted by frascas. (Indeed, writing a guidebook of all the current frascas in existence could make a nice retirement project. . . .)

This book is a dedication to the Friulano frasca and its food and wine. The recipes herein reflect the food we have been enjoying over more than fifteen years of visits to Friuli, along with many of the dishes that we serve at our own frasca in Boulder.

Our restaurant has been open since 2004, and that we are still open and still vibrant so many years later is already lucky. Even with my knowledge of wine (which I explore in the first chapter) and Lachlan's expertise in the kitchen, we recognize that a lot of our success is because we chose Friuli as our beacon. We didn't realize it back then but our restaurant is richer in depth, our guests happier, and our employees more inspired because we decided to hang our hat on Friuli Venezia Giulia. Nightly in our dining room, we talk to guests who want to experience the "undiscovered" Italy. Friuli is that place. We hope you make a pilgrimage to Friuli, like we did in the beginning, using this book as your muse. But if you are unable to visit, we've structured the information here so you can create your own frasca at home, with an introduction to the region's wines followed by recipes that will situate you, spiritually and flavorfully, in the heart of Friuli.

Wine

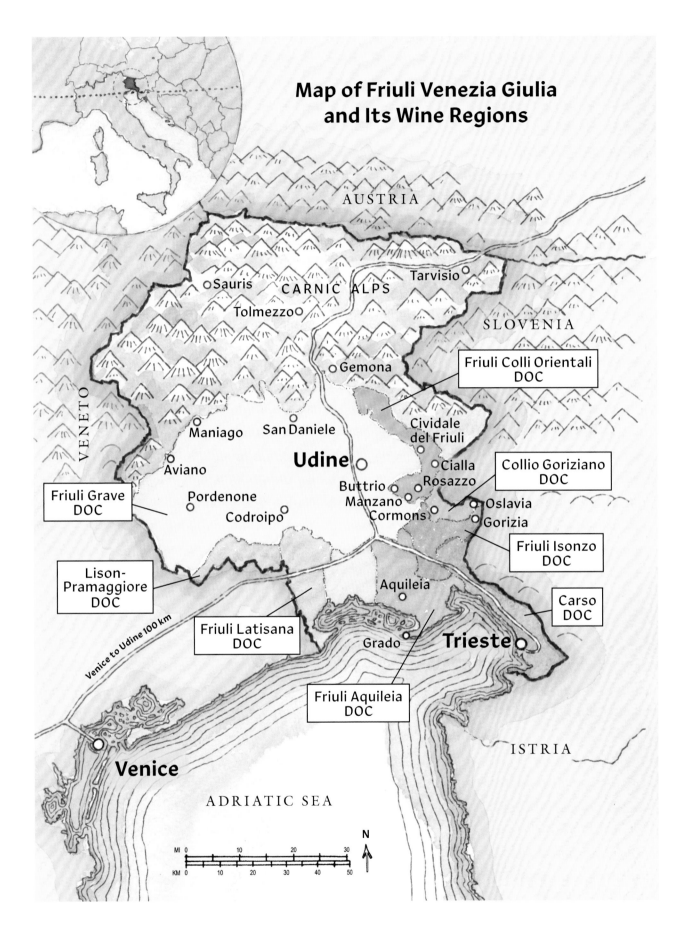

Map of Friuli Venezia Giulia and Its Wine Regions

AUSTRIA

CARNIC ALPS

Tarvisio

Sauris

Tolmezzo

SLOVENIA

Gemona

Friuli Colli Orientali
DOC

Cividale
del Friuli

VENETO

Maniago

San Daniele

Udine

Cialla
Rosazzo

Collio Goriziano
DOC

Friuli Grave
DOC

Aviano

Pordenone

Codroipo

Buttrio
Manzano
Cormons

Oslavia

Gorizia

Friuli Isonzo
DOC

Lison-
Pramaggiore
DOC

Aquileia

Carso
DOC

Friuli Latisana
DOC

Venice to Udine 100 km

Grado

Trieste

Friuli Aquileia
DOC

ISTRIA

Venice

ADRIATIC SEA

MI 0   10   20   30

KM 0 10 20 30 40 50

N

The Terroir of Friuli Venezia Giulia

As someone who has spent my adult life working in restaurants and the last twenty-five-plus years as a sommelier, I have had the chance to visit countless wineries all over the world. I can honestly say that no wine region offers as much diversity as Friuli Venezia Giulia (FVG). The sheer number of different grapes, the styles of wine produced, the dizzying variety of winemaking philosophies behind them . . . how is this even possible?

Friuli Venezia Giulia enjoys a rich terroir that is defined by the diversity of its landscapes. Nestled between mountains (the Carnic and Julian Alps) and sea (the Adriatic), Friuli's singular position exposes the region to varying weather patterns that, when combined with a high concentration of *ponca* soil (a mix of marl, sandstone, and ancient oceanic sediment; see image on page 44), create a unique alchemy. At the southern edge of FVG lies the northernmost sandy beaches of the Adriatic Sea, which meld into the coastal town of Trieste. As you can see from the map on the facing page, Trieste is less than ninety-five kilometers from the Carnic Alps and Julian Alps, which separate Friuli from southern Austria and Slovenia, respectively. This means you have land rising up from sea level to alluvial plain and hillside levels well within that zone. This kind of geography results in two hillside Denominazione di Origine Controllata (DOC) wine regions, Friuli Colli Orientali and Collio Goriziano, and six flatland DOCs, Carso, Lison-Pramaggiore, Friuli Latisana, Friuli Grave, Friuli Aquileia, and Friuli Isonzo.

In FVG, southern winds gather the warmth of the Adriatic and meet the famous (and gusty) bora wind that descends over the Alps heading toward the coast. If you visit the Collio Goriziano and/or Colli Orientali and stand between the hills of Rosazzo and Buttrio, you can actually feel the cool air from the Carnic Alps in the north, the heat from Croatia in the south, and the exposure of the sun on the soil. It's immediate and it's wild. And this situation is important for understanding the terroir, because the winds keep the vineyards cooler during sunny spells, which gives the grapes a longer growing season. Actually, these grapes have a longer season than grapes in any other region of Italy, including those that grow in cooler climates such as the Alto-Adige or the Veneto. The length of the growing season affects the acidity of the grapes, which in turn affects *verticality* (an upright, thirst-quenching wine—meaning it has a high drinkability—with a well-balanced natural sugar content and a host of other variables that we will explore in the varietal section that follows).

Whether it's the gravel pebbles you find in the Friuli Grave DOC or the ponca in the Collio region, soil plays a key role in Friulano terroir. In the wine world, we talk a lot about the great Kimmeridgian soils of Chablis—the benchmark for how soil is expressed in wine—and how the mix of limestone, clay, and fossilized oyster shells brings minerality to Chablis' Chardonnay grape. In FVG, you find lighter soils in the Grave wine region, which result in a lighter-bodied white wine. But as you move east through Udine into the Colli Orientali, the soil changes into ponca. And so here, you taste salt from the sea but still get a full-bodied white. The poverty of the ponca soil naturally stresses the vines, which yield relatively small quantities of grapes while providing a distinctive minerality.

How to Visit a Friulano Winery

Visiting a winery in Friuli is nothing like wine-tasting in Sonoma County or Napa Valley, where each winery has a tasting room and a staff to take care of you when you drop in. In Friuli, you make an appointment with the winery owner or a family member, and you often end up having that appointment in their living room or cellar. You do not have to be a wine professional to make an appointment; you simply must be a wine enthusiast. Most of the wineries do have a webpage, so you can set up an appointment ahead of time. Visits are usually scheduled around the flow of the winery's workday and chores. For example, when I visit Enzo Pontoni at Miani, the appointment is either at noon or 4 p.m., based on when Enzo takes a break from working in the vineyards. This is typical, because the wineries are small, family-run businesses. This is also what is so magical, so be sure to be on time!

Friuli is much easier to explore today than it was fifteen years ago when Lachlan; Nate Ready; my wife, Danette; and I were driving with our maps out, often feeling carsick, trying to find a road that didn't appear in print. Now there are all kinds of online maps and any number of GPS devices to guide you. Tools notwithstanding, it takes more time to get around Friuli than you think it will, so always give yourself a buffer of twenty minutes (at least). . . .

If the stars align, and you are able to schedule appointments very close to one another location-wise, it is possible to visit three wineries in one day. That being said, I recommend keeping it to two appointments in one wine zone, with plenty of time in between; for example, one at 10 a.m. and the second at 2:30 p.m. in the Carso. You may be thinking, "No way, I can get it all done!" But you really should be leaving room for a chance at the "Friuli vortex," which would be excruciating if you were overcommitted but is an incredible life experience if you've left yourself some time. The Friuli vortex occurs when the morning appointment leads to an invitation to eat lunch with the family or head into the vineyards to drink wine and taste their homemade salami and cheese, or an afternoon appointment leads to aperitivo.

To illustrate, as I write this section of the book, we are currently in Friuli. We began the day at Gravner and arrived on time to Saša Radikon's. But then Saša's mother made us a brodo with semolina dumplings (which is somewhat similar to our canederli recipe on page 213), and Saša opened a selection of their 1995 bottling, and a few bottles more, and . . . we were late for our next appointment. (Mind you, the two vineyards we were visiting are only 300 yards apart, but this is what is considered a great experience of the Friulano vortex; the opportunity to be with a great family, like Saša in his home.) These moments are not common occurrences in any of our lives, so you want to be flexible enough to do it. Maybe not every appointment ends in a positive vortex, but when it does, it's priceless. Schedule your next day in a different DOC. And use "Our Friuli Address Book" on page 252 to find a great lunch spot somewhere along the way.

But be aware that all of the restaurants in FVG are closed on different days. For example, if you try to book La Subida (see page 94) on a Tuesday or Wednesday, you will be out of luck, because the restaurant is closed. When planning your itinerary, always check the (customized) weekly closing dates of restaurants.

Dissection of a Wine Label

PRODOTTO IN ITALIA · CONTIENE SOLFITI · CONTAINS SULPHITES · ENTHÄLT SULFITE · L 2

Imbottigliato
all'origine dalla
Azienda Agricola
Borgo del Tiglio
di Nicola Manferrari
Cormòns - I - Italia

COLLIO
Denominazione
di Origine Controllata

RONCO
DELLA CHIESA
2 0 1 7

0,75 ℓ e   13,5% vol

BORGO
DEL TIGLIO

Producer

Wine Region

Vintage Year

Alcohol Content

It's completely puzzling to me that, to this day, in most wine books, even *Italian* wine books, FVG is lumped together with Trentino–Alto Adige and Veneto in one "Northeast Italy" section. That's essentially like combining the Loire, Burgundy, and Beaujolais into one homogenous chapter! In truth, FVG is like no other wine region. When I was living in Napa Valley and visited producers, I discovered that many made Cabernet very similarly. They used the same kinds of barrels, and even the same consultants or winemakers. Friuli is not like that. On the same day, on the same road, you might meet a producer making a Tocai Friulano in a crispy, non-oxidative style. His neighbor might make it with a lot of *bâtonnage* (meaning the lees are stirred by hand) and malolactic fermentation (bacteria conversion), which is very powerful when combined with French oak. The next producer might use no oak, and another might make a macerated wine. They're all living in the same vicinity, but each has a different point of view. Very rarely do you encounter that much variety in any other wine region. In fact, very few regions can handle that many winemaking styles. In FVG, they're all appropriate, and they're all correct.

The White Wine Grapes of FVG

On any given day in Friuli, you might find producers who ferment their white wine in stainless-steel tanks, small oak barrels, clay amphorae (yes, just like in Mesopotamia), cement dairy tanks, or large upright wood barrels. You can visit three winemakers in the same small area and each will have completely different approaches to the same grapes from the same vicinity. What's even more amazing is that all of the wines are delicious. While visiting Burgundy or Bordeaux, or any other classic wine region really, you may taste very different wines, but each of these regions has an overarching style of winemaking; there might be some subtle stylistic differences based on individual talent, but the format varies little.

Friuli, by contrast, is home to a dizzying number of different grapes. It is a complex patchwork of varietals, vineyards, cultures, and ideas. In the list of varietals that follows, you may know of and tried a few, but others you will never have heard of simply because you never see these wines outside of a tiny corner in this magical place. Each varietal has its own section that is followed by a fitting example of a wine of that varietal from a producer who really makes the grape shine. I have included the producers' names, the area where the vineyards are located, and the Denominazione di Origine Controllata (DOC). I have also included a short profile of each producer, because often the best way to learn and understand a wine is to know the man or woman behind it. That's the hook. And, with the exception of one or two, all of these wines are available in the United States if you choose to seek them out.

Ruttars, Gorizia

FRIULANO, AKA TOCAI

Friulano is a varietal that symbolizes more to Friuli than any other, ergo it is the first varietal I wanted to address. The name means "the grape of here," and while that would seem to describe the grape perfectly, it has only had the simple Friulano moniker since 2007; before then, it was known as Tocai Friulano (and as Tokaji, across the fence in Slovenia). When Hungary joined the European Union, Hungarian winemakers successfully lobbied the EU for the exclusive rights to the Tokaji appellation. (Even though the Tocai grape doesn't exist in Hungary—in the Tokaji appellation, the grapes are called Hárslevel˝u, Kövérsz˝ol˝o, and Furmint!) This is how the varietal known as Friulano came to be, and also how, in France, Tokay d'Alsace became Pinot Gris. The changes have been painful for everyone in Friuli; you may still see a sign in some bars with an X marked through Friulano and a heart drawn next to Tocai.

Friulano has phenomenal range: it can be crisp and quaffable—the quintessential porch-pounder when grown on the lighter soils of the Friuli Grave DOC—and it can reach to large, powerful high-extract weight when it comes from the Collio area. It's the varietal that Mother Nature most likely created to accompany a slice of prosciutto di San Daniele. For hundreds of years, Tocai Friulano was the region's indigenous grape and the building block at the dinner table in Friuli.

This grape is really woven into the fabric of daily life in Friuli; two mechanics in an Udinese *osteria* (tavern) might drink a *tajùt* (a "cut" of wine) on their morning break, or it could be paired with radicchio at lunch, or poured at a Michelin-starred restaurant such as La Subida for dinner. Very few varietals, for the price, enjoy this kind of range. (In Friuli you can walk into Canteen Rauscedo and fill up a vessel of your choosing with Friulano for 1 euro per liter, or about $1.15 per quart. How often are you happy to knock back a glass of two-buck Chardonnay? Probably never.) Friulano can be enjoyed in a garage or at the opera; it can handle wood, but it doesn't need it; it has minerality, but it isn't too racy. What do I mean by "too racy"? Think of Chablis, which makes you constantly thirsty for more Chablis. On the other end of the spectrum, think of a white Rhône that's like olive oil—Friulano naturally has extract and power, but it's not too oily. For rich dishes, like polenta, frico, or risotto, you need a wine that has that shoulder for you to cuddle up to.

Friulano is to Friuli as Grüner Veltliner is to Austria. Grüner, like Friulano, is versatile. In the Kamptal wine region, you could drink a Bründlmayer Lamm, a powerful, heady, age-worthy Grüner—similar to Corton-Charlemagne—or you could quaff a Domäne Wachau Federspiel Terrassen, all elegance and light body. Available at two wildly different price points, both wines perform their job of translating the grape admirably well. In other words, there's nothing wrong with enjoying an honest Tuesday-night dinner with a crisp, refreshing Friulano from Rasceudo's cooperative. Or you could drink Ronco della Chiesa Bianco from Borgo del Tiglio, with tasting notes of white strawberries and cream and marzipan. These wines show the incredible bell curve of one grape varietal that's powerful enough to be a grand cru wine at a Michelin-starred restaurant.

Miani
Buttrio, Udine
Colli Orientali

Winemaker Enzo Pontoni (pictured on page 20) of Miani wine fame is a gruff, striking farmer with piercing blue eyes. He can almost always be found working in his garage/barn, tinkering on tractors or other vineyard-management equipment. Sure, he is a world-class winemaker, but he is also one of the best vineyard farmers in Italy. A rugged gentleman outdoorsman, he's actually a peaceful, soft-spoken man and one of the hardest-working farmers in all of the wine regions I have visited. He makes powerful, but not monolithic, wines; wines with great extract and distilled drinkability—one of the hardest things to get right.

Enzo represents a farmer-first mentality, crafting great wine through thirty-plus years in the vineyards. And he is *always* in those vineyards. Enzo took over from his father in 1991. Here is someone who makes the most expensive wine in Italy and still refers to Friulano as Tocai. Though I've known him for years, I can't even be sure he realizes the world is clamoring for his wines. (For those who can't get one allocation of Miani, enthusiasts are trading it on the grey market for ten times what it costs when it leaves the cellar.)

Enzo also works with Ribolla, Sauvignon, and Refosco grapes. In many others' hands, on the same slopes of Buttrio, these wines become too concentrated or too "hot," as we say in the wine world; that is, too alcoholic or too monolithic. For instance, the 2015 vintage was very ripe, but Miani still had all the bells and whistles (a lot of ripeness, extract, aromatics, power). This is not easy winemaking, and Enzo has a deft touch that has gained him well-deserved fame. If you haven't had Miani white wines before, they are similar to a great Hermitage Blanc from the Rhône but with more structure.

Borgo del Tiglio
Brazzano, Gorizia
Collio Goriziano

At this winery toils Nicola Manferrari (pictured at left), a pharmacist who took over his parents' vineyard after the death of his father in the early 1980s. Historically, Borgo del Tiglio made wine for local osterie and wine bars. Every once in a while, you can still come across an osteria, such as Al Cappello in Udine, that pours Borgo del Tiglio wine by the demijohn (and if you do, stay awhile).

Nicola had a different vision than his father, however; he wanted to make white wine in the same league as a great white Burgundy: world-class, lightly oak-aged, and vinified along the same principles. Today, his Ronco della Chiesa vineyard is considered the Montrachet of Tocai Friulano, the best single vineyard for the grape. The vineyard is an old, funky parcel on the base slopes of Mount Quarin, a chapel-topped mountainside that rolls right into the backyard of Nicola's house. While Enzo Pontoni at Miani is a farmer first and foremost, crafting great wine through long hours in the vineyard, Nicola Manferrari is more focused on special vineyard parcels that allow a beautiful expression of the grapes. His wine has aromas of white strawberries and hay and finishes with a bitter, green almond note that begs you to drink more. It has power, but isn't too much.

Enzo Pontoni of Miani

Winemakers to Watch

Mitja Sirk (pictured at right), a sommelier and member of the Sirk family who owns La Subida (see page 94), started making his own Friulano from Collio vines in 2017. His Bianco is crisp, delicious, and highly drinkable. Frasca Food and Wine sommelier Matt Mather named it his favorite Friulano of the 2017 vintage.

Christian Patat, of Ronco del Gnemiz, is working with the sons of his wife, Serena Palazzolo, on a vineyard management team to take over two old estates they'll call Le Due Monte, producing Chardonnay, Sauvignon Blanc, and Friulano with a very refined touch.

Luca Belluzzo hails from the village of Tarcento way up in the northern part of the Colli Orientali. His family is bottling tiny amounts of fantastic Refosco from their high-altitude vineyards.

Marco Pinat from Povoletto is a great young producer whose first vintage was 2015, making Refosco and Friulano from his Colli Orientali site along with a dry Verduzzo.

His are wines that can age very gracefully. The Gran Selezione monovarietal whites, particularly the Sauvignon and Malvasia, are incredible. Manferrari will only make them in great vintages; they are powerful but incredibly age-worthy. The Sauvignon Selezione is reminiscent of a wonderful Graves Blanc. Borgo del Tiglio also produces a very small amount of Collio Rosso wine from Merlot and Cabernet Franc. It is a quintessential Friulano Merlot with intense, deep red-apple-skin aroma. There is just enough ripe fruit to please the senses, but not enough to overshadow the mineral and earthy aromas that are distinctly Old World. This is a very special wine.

With Nicola, you can show up for a wine-tasting appointment, stay for twenty minutes, and then it's time to go. Or you might receive an in-depth tutorial about pruning while on an exhaustive tour of his vineyard site, followed by a vertical tasting of thirty-some vintages (see "How to Visit a Friulano Winery," page 14). You never really know what kind of visit you're going to get. It could be a footnote. Or it could be a highlight of your career.

Raccaro
Near Cormòns, Gorizia
Collio Goriziano

In the same neighborhood as Borgo del Tiglio, just a couple of streets down but on the same slope, you'll find Raccaro. If you were to bump into Dario Raccaro on a Sunday night at Enoteca di Cormòns after he's had a few tajùts, your evening will have just gotten much better. "Passionate," "powerful," and "volcanic" are words that describe Dario and his wines. He happens to have vineyards on Vigna del Rolat, the same great land exposition to the sun as Nicola Manferrari. His Vigna del Rolat Friulano has aromas of perfectly ripe pineapple. It is incredibly powerful, but with no oak.

A lot of us think "no oak, no power," but Raccaro's wines exemplify the contrary. Many people across the globe who are now playing around with Chardonnay (or other full-bodied whites in steel tanks) could learn a lot from Dario Raccaro, and how he makes a powerful but finessed, drinkable Friuliano with no wood. You may even start to notice, when you're visiting cellars around Friuli, that Raccaro is a producer that the other producers in the area consistently collect (that is, their cellars are full of it)—he's clearly the benchmark producer of powerful, unoaked Friulano for the Collio.

SAUVIGNON BLANC

Sauvignon Blanc is the gateway for FVG whites because the wine appeals to so many people in so many different ways. Sommeliers love it, but so does everyone else. But why are we discussing a varietal that's native to France and that we associate with Sancerre and Pouilly-Fumé? The grape showed up in FVG in the 1800s, and it has two possible origin stories. Some think Napoleon brought it along with his cavalry; others believe that a French noblewoman married a Friulano aristocrat, bringing some vines with her. Regardless, the story of Sauvignon Blanc is one of successful adaptation: it naturally sets low yields and the grape clusters are more of a loosely bunched oval, which allows for nice air flow in a moist locale. This clone is set up for success thanks to the Alpine diurnal temperatures, the sea, the mountain, and the crosswinds—these give Sauvignon Blanc an extra gearbox.

Classic Sauvignon Blanc is a showcase for a trilogy of citruses: lemon, lime, and grapefruit. It also has grassy and herbaceous notes. When winemaker Didier Dagueneau came onto the Loire Valley scene in the 1980s, he created a Sauvignon Blanc that had a fuller mouthfeel and extract. His Pouilly-Fumés had a different level of flavor, aromatics, and structure; his was a more complex expression of the grapes, and Americans had never tasted it before. I still remember the first time I tried a Dagueneau wine in the 1990s; the Pouilly-Fumé was truly extraordinary, still 100 percent Sauvignon Blanc but with a different power and structure. Other winemakers in the Loire have been trying to chase the dragon of Didier Dagueneau ever since.

The next Dagueneau is not in the Loire but rather over in northeast Italy. Many great producers in Friuli can extract a balance of aromatics, apricot, and peach but still be wonderfully precise with acidity. That vibrancy or mouthwatering acidity is what makes Sauvignon Blanc tremendously drinkable. It's not uncommon to find a 14 percent Sauvignon Blanc in the Colli Orientali that still has 6 grams of acid per liter (in the Loire Valley, it would be 12 percent Sauvignon Blanc). Sauvignon Blanc is tricky, though, in that it has a very tight window in which it needs to be picked. As ripeness increases and potential alcohol rises, there comes a moment when the acidity drops rapidly; winemakers have to nail that knife-edge balance to produce a Sauvignon Blanc with spine, ripeness, and acidity. In FVG, Sauvignon Blanc grapes creep rather than race to ripeness. You see your favorite Napa winemakers picking in the last week of July or the first week of August. That's much earlier than the first week of September in FVG, though the grapes likely budded at the same time in both regions. This difference explains how Sauvignon Blanc vintages in FVG can often be fresh and ripe and have verticality in more bountiful, and therefore more accessible, amounts.

Ronco del Gnemiz
Near San Giovanni al Natisone, Udine
Colli Orientali

Full disclosure: Serena Palazzolo and her partner, Christian Patat (who is pictured on the facing page), are very close to my heart. We've enjoyed countless bottles of Champagne and old Friulano together. Serena has been like a big sister to Frasca Food and Wine, housing many of our employees over the years to work the harvest.

Serena's father bought the Ronco del Gnemiz vineyard in 1964 and had his first bottling in 1981. Serena joined the family business in 1985, and Christian, the Giulio Gambelli of white wine and a master taster, arrived in 2001. (Gambelli was a maestro of Tuscan wines, and a big believer in the power of the Sangiovese grape, which he sought to raise from relative obscurity. He managed this with great success at houses such as Soldera, Montevertine, Poggio di Sotto, Ormanni, and Il Colle.) Serena and Christian make the next great Sauvignon Blanc, in my opinion. Their Sauvignon Sol and Sauvignon Peri, and one from their newest site, Salici, are all great expressions of the grape. They can become powerful while ripening until the last possible moment on the hills of Rosazzo, but they never lack drinkability. Many Frasca guests ask for a second bottle of Ronco del Gnemiz's iconic, crazy-ripe 2013 Peri.

These amazing Sauvignon Blancs also dispel the myth that white wines from Italy cannot age. In fact, these wines need a little time after release to shed their chiseled minerality. Age these from six months to one year after release and you'll see a completely different wine. "We always felt that Sauvignon Blanc is meant to grow in Friuli. The grape is very reactive to the soil and the clay and, simply put, for us it is the secret weapon of Friuli," Christian told me one day. Friuli pushes the end of the season, taking four to five weeks longer to get that ripeness. This leaves roughly five days to pick. Picking at the right moment is key; you're looking to surpass the grassy notes, have a hint of citrus, and cruise into that bruised-peach zone.

Venica & Venica
Near Dolegna del Collio, Gorizia
Collio Goriziano

The Venica family has been living on their little street outside of Dolegna in the northern part of the Collio for four generations. The family singlehandedly turned many people in the United States and France onto the bright, crisp, but very complex Sauvignon Blanc from their Ronco delle Mele vineyard—on such a steep, north-facing slope that the grandfather planted apple trees to slow erosion and prevent mudslides in the rainy season.

Giampaolo Venica's father and uncle have been running the winery since the 1970s. I first met Giampaolo in 1997, when he, sporting a ponytail, was an intern working for Jim Clendenen at the Au Bon Climat winery in Santa Barbara. We ate Mexican food and drank magnums of well-aged wine (that's how people had

Wine Drinker Alert: Fruilian Whites Are for Aging, Friulian Whites Are Forever!

We grow up thinking that Italian red wines can be age-worthy and collectable, while white wines should be consumed upon release. I have often heard people say, "What's the deal with these older vintage whites, shouldn't I want something fresher?" Sure, if you're on the Amalfi Coast drinking Greco or in Piedmont knocking back some Arneis, I see your point. But the whites in FVG are meant to age. We have ripped into a current release countless times at Frasca Food and Wine and thought, "Oops! Let's put that back in the cellar, it's not ready to drink yet," because the wine is too shy and not showing its personality (just as we do with white Burgundy, white Alsace, or white Bordeaux).

One of my favorite memories is leading a trip of sommeliers to FVG in 2010 and blind-tasting a twenty-year-old Venica Pinot Blanc with Giampaolo Venica. Some of the best minds in wine could not wrap their heads around it (fully alive, framed with great acidity). In 2016, I helped Andrea Felluga lead a tasting of the Livio Felluga Terre Alte, going back twenty vintages, and I remember the bewilderment and conversations those wines sparked. Everyone at that tasting realized that, when aged, FVG whites can be like great Burgundy wines.

This is why I love blind-tasting wines. Preconceived notions are never your friend. If you bring your wine baggage to the table, you will have less fun and, more important, you will not learn.

---

lunch at ABC back then). We've been friends ever since. And now he is back at the winery, pitching in wherever the family needs and generally just being a great ambassador for Sauvignon Blanc and Friuli as a whole.

The style of the Venicas' Sauvignon Blanc? No wood or stainless steel; it is hyper-aromatic, hyper-fresh, and herbaceous. It could be mistaken for a great Sancerre if blind-tasted. Compared to Gnemiz, for example, Venica tends to be a bit more grassy; whereas Gnemiz has a haunting of wood. When I was working at the Little Nell restaurant in Aspen in the mid-1990s, Venica was one of the first Sauvignon Blancs that caught my eye. When I visit friend and co-author Meredith in Montreal, Venica is on almost all of the city's best wine lists. (More on Venica when we discuss Malvasia on page 33.)

PINOT GRIGIO

Not a night goes by while I'm working the restaurant floor without a customer saying, "I'd love a great glass of Pinot Grigio." Now, many a sommelier might, at this point, admit to rolling their eyes, hustling back to the wine cooler, and wanting desperately to instead grab the trendy white of the moment—a Grüner, Assyrtiko, and so on. But in fact, a request for Pinot Grigio is great hospitality practice for sommeliers.

Yes, Pinot Grigio suffered from its own success in the 1980s and '90s, when it became a watered-down commodity. Many of us still remember Joan Collins and Linda Evans on *Dynasty* rocking a huge glass of white wine with ice. But just

Venica & Venica Vineyards

like Pinot Gris in Alsace (one of only four varieties you can grow on a grand cru plot, and grand cru wines must be single varietal, coming from a single vineyard), Pinot Grigio has the potential to be an incredible vehicle of terroir, as long as it's planted in the right sites. When you plant Pinot Grigio in the ponca soil of Friuli, you might find yourself with a wine presenting lip-smacking acidity and great melon fruit, wrapped up in the salinity for which ponca is known. The terroir makes an incredible food wine, delicious with raw fish or *spaghetti alle vongole*. Pinot Grigio is in fact a noble grape, one that communicates its terroir. When you order a bottle of Chablis, it has to reflect the Kimmeridge clay soil. If you order a bottle of Beaujolais, the Gamay grape needs to taste of granite. If it's Mosel Riesling, it needs to taste of blue slate. And, if it's Pinot Grigio from the Collio, it has to have the salinity of ponca soil. And *that* is what makes a wine noble . . . *not how expensive it is.*

Many people don't realize that Pinot Grigio is a mutation of Pinot Noir, a red grape. So, if you have low-yielding Pinot Grigio and give it a little time on the skin, you end up with a beautiful, rosy pinkish salmon color—not as dark as rosé, and not as brilliant as white wine. The Scarbolo family does this fantastically well at their winery, turning out a rosy pink, textured, full-bodied Pinot Grigio that people love (and a nice alternative for those who like California Chard but want to try something more "exotic").

There's an area of the Collio that I like to call the Banana Belt. When zooming down from the very cold Colli Orientali on a bike ride with Lachlan and Craig Lewis, a former-pro-cyclist friend of ours, we made a left turn at the hamlet of Ruttars, heading toward the border town of Plessiva, and could just feel the climate getting a little warmer. More than eighty years ago, a great freeze killed many of the olive trees in Friuli, specifically in the Collio, but none of the vines. In that area, you find many great producers of Pinot Grigio, including Franco Toros, Aldo Polencic, and Edi Keber (see page 29). Wines here tend to get riper, fuller, and richer. Aldo Polencic is a case study for a powerful, rich, and full-bodied Pinot Grigio, and a perfect wine to accompany fritto misto (see page 162) or bagna cauda and aioli.

In Friuli, when you enter a frasca, someone pours you a *tajùt*, a "cut" of wine, and historically it is Tocai Friulano. On Frasca Food and Wine's opening night, I thought, "Let's tajùt somebody, and if they come back, we'll continue to tajùt them." Flash forward two years and we had a lot of regulars, which meant a lot of tajùt-ing, translating to cases of wine a week.

In 2006, on a trip to Friuli with Lachlan and our staff to fine-tune Frasca's food, we approached Christian Patat and Serena Palazollo from Ronco del Gnemiz winery (see page 23) and asked them to make a Tocai Friulano that we could pour at Frasca as a tajùt for all guests. They did, and the tajùt became the hall-mark of Frasca hospitality.

Livio Felluga
Near Brazzano di Cormons, Gorizia
Colli Orientali

A good example of nobility are the wines of Livio Felluga. We wouldn't have started Frasca Food and Wine, nor would we have written this book, were it not for Livio Felluga. Because he and his pioneering spirit are really what put Friuli on the map. Historically, members of his family were wine merchants in Grado on the coast. After the Second World War, Livio wanted to become a winemaker. He moved to the hills of Rosazzo—when everyone was leaving the area to find work elsewhere—and became the caretaker and owner of some of the greatest vineyards in the Collio and Colli Orientali, many of them on steep slopes. Today, the Felluga family makes not just affordable and delicious wines such as Sauvignon Blanc and Pinot Grigio but also *vins de garde* (that is, wines meant for aging, or wines meant for collecting) such as their world-class Terre Alte, a white blend that showcases the longevity of Friulano whites. They are also now the caretakers of the historic cellars and vineyards of the Rosazzo abbey, making a white blend there that is the archetype for the new white DOCG, Rosazzo Bianco. On the grounds of the *abbazia* (abbey), the last remaining vines of Pignolo (see page 46) were discovered. Livio Felluga is universally acknowledged as the estate that reestablished Friuli's winemaking heritage.

But why is their Pinot Grigio so good? Well, some of the world's best Pinot Grigios in general come from northern Italy, and the varietal favors the cooler climates of the Veneto and Friuli. The Felluga family has worked very hard and invested in the region for the last sixty years; and in so doing, they have developed a quiver of fantastic sites for Pinot Grigio that enjoy some of the greatest climatic conditions of Friuli. Felluga wines are known to be crisp and refreshing with hints of citrus and great minerality. This is a family that takes the process of making a $15 wine very seriously.

PINOT BIANCO

This varietal originally came to Friuli from France. Pinot Blanc in France is a quaffable, delicious white wine from Alsace. In Alsace, it's a porch-pounder that's not considered for grand cru status. In Italy, you see it throughout the Alto Adige, with a small amount planted in Friuli, and what is here is, for the most part, stunning. In the Collio, specifically, there is great representation. It has a huge window of drinkability, meaning it drinks well in its youth but also with age. In its youth, it has really crispy, delicious apple notes, and is somewhat full-bodied but not flabby. Where Meursault doesn't lend itself to easy drinking, Pinot Bianco does. It's a perfectly beautiful expression of the grape, tasting of ripe delicious red apple and pear with wonderful citrus notes. These are the kinds of flavors we usually find in a full-bodied Pinot Blanc from Alsace.

The Keber vineyard lies just two minutes away from the Slovenian border. The family has been farming this land for 350 years and bottling wine since 1957, and the winery went organic in 2012. With Edi's son Kristian now at the helm, the winery makes just one wine, a Collio Bianco. This is a proud blend of three native Collio grapes: Friulano (for body and structure), Malvasia Istriana (for salinity, minerality, and aroma), and Ribolla Gialla (for acidity); across the border in Slovenia, they also make a Brda (the Slovenian name for Collio) white in the tiny hilltop village of Medana. Edi Keber's Collio Bianco is always a full-bodied and rich, but not oaked, white wine. It's something that you don't see much in the Napa Valley, where the rich, powerful wines have oak inflection. This is all about the vineyard. The Friulano speaks beautifully with aromatics of white strawberry, stone fruits, and a little bit of toasted bitter almond.

In the wine world, blending is a way to diversify your assets and protect you from bad years—hail, rain, and the like are all great ways for farmers to starve! The Collio is one of the rainiest areas in Italy (with nearly 80 inches annually). And so, until the 1970s, almost everyone was blending. Come the 1980s, though, the trend for varietal wines kicked into overdrive. Many producers diversified by buying different vineyards in different locations.

The Kebers decided to develop a distinct, easily recognizable bottle for their Collio Bianco (like Barolo or Barbaresco have their own Albeisa bottle); it has a more defined neck and looks slightly square. The microclimate of this area is very warm—we are in what Lachlan and I like to refer to as the Banana Belt; as soon as you physically enter the zone (which we do often as it is around the corner from La Subida, where we love to stay), the wind dies and it feels like the tropics—which perhaps explains why Kristian Keber is always wearing a (Slayer) T-shirt while working his vineyards.

VITOVSKA

This varietal lives on a wild and brushy escarpment a rock's throw from Trieste, a little more than three kilometers from the beach. While it's so very close to the northern shores of the Adriatic, it couldn't feel farther away in a sense. The combination of the bora wind from the northeast and the incredibly difficult conditions in which the winemakers live create extreme winemaking conditions. However, if you were to ask me about a varietal that denotes the Carso DOC (named after the karst soil, a mix of limestone, dolomite, and gypsum) from all others, it would have to be Vitovska. It is 100 percent the most important grape of the Carso, though it does have a red colleague, Terrano, which we discuss later. Talk about a wine of place. Not only is it a wine just of Friuli, but it's also really a varietal just of the Carso. You don't see it in other parts of Friuli, and you definitely don't see it in other parts of Italy.

Vodopivec
Near Sgonico, Trieste
Carso

*The terra-cotta amphorae
at Vodopivec*

To understand Vitovska, you can talk to only one person: Paolo Vodopivec (pictured at right). This square-jawed rustic farmer will tell you that Vitovska is queen of the Carso, "the land of stone and wind," and able to grow in very difficult conditions. Paolo would know, as his family has been in this part of the Carso since 1632. In 1997, Paolo decided to transform his *agriturismo* (farm-stay) from trading in cheese, pigs, and flowers to making only Vitovska wines. Since then, he has focused on just one grape; I cannot think of another winemaker who has mastered one varietal in the last decade. Paolo isn't hedging his bets with diversity; but rather, he makes faultless world-class wine in a style that is historically hard to do.

At 260 meters of elevation, Vodopivec is just north of the village of Prosecco. The small vineyards are surrounded by other flora and fauna. The vines are individually laid, which means each vineyard is its own ecosystem, surrounded by the brush of the Carso. Paolo says his vineyard is deliberately natural and that Vitovska is the best vehicle to show the character of the land. The Carso has a very unique and interesting soil; basically a thin, poor layer of organic topsoil with a patchwork of granite and iron underneath. If you were to take a quarter cut of the earth like a slice of pie, you'd be amazed to see the determination of those vines as they find every little gap between the rock. Driving by, you'd think you were in a quarry, not a vineyard. Or maybe even a sinkhole (for which the area is famous).

Paolo has changed a lot of his processes over the last ten years. The first time I visited in 2007, he was experimenting with terra-cotta amphorae, which he laid out in his front yard like geranium pots. By 2017, his cellar felt like a temple or a monastery. Those pots are now in the cellar and look something like alien pods. After visiting thousands of wineries, I am genuinely moved by Vodopivec. Mystical, relevant, and in tune with many of the great winemakers I've met, the man and his place are poetic.

Wine-wise, where does he fall within Friuli? Well, yes, the wines are macerated, but they aren't orange (see page 40). They're Vitovska first, Carso second, Vodopivec third, and macerated fourth. Some have been macerated for up to a year on their skins in amphorae. But the wines are clear and vibrant in tension, quite luminescent, and completely indicative of the terroir. This is white wine with a lot of application; I could drink this with a whole branzino (see page 169), and at the same time, I could see it complementing a pork shank. This is absolutely a wine for the table. Now, there isn't a lot of it out there in the world, so for those of you who haven't tried it—which is most of you—what does it taste like? It's shy and a great example of minerality; light. It doesn't really have a counterpart.

MALVASIA ISTRIANA

"Anyone that's crazy for terroir should be crazy for Malvasia."

—Giampaolo Venica

Doro Princic
Near Cormons, Gorizia
Collio Goriziano

This is the greatest of the Malvasia clones. Why do I say *clones* plural? Because Malvasia is found all over the Adriatic and Mediterranean—from Spain to Greece to Italy. The bad news is that those clones don't necessarily translate to flavor; many are fruity and aromatic but kind of clumsy with acidity. The one exception is the Istriana clone that has found its way into the white, light soils of Istria and on up into the more powerful ponca soils of Friuli. This is where this grape achieves its fullest potential and becomes one of the greatest fish/seafood wines in the world, which makes sense, as Venice merchants first brought the original Malvasia vines from Greece. It's floral, it's minerally, and it has almost a saltiness to it. I crave it with whole fish or Risotto Marinara (page 159).

If you're a fan of French whites such as Viognier, Marsanne, and Roussanne, you will be enamored with this grape. It has the same aromatics but trades in a little bit of that Liberace flash for a dash of salinity and minerality that the very famous white Rhônes lack, and for a precise kind of acidity of which Viognier, Marsanne, and Roussanne can only dream.

As Giampaolo Venica (pictured at left) says, "I think both my Malvasia Istriana Petris and the single-vineyard Friulano Ronco delle Cime have this quality similar to a rocky Chablis with steady salinity; it feels like I am driving down into Trieste smelling iodine or driving on the long bridge in Grado, surrounded by the *laguna* [lagoon]. Some deep but not heavy algae salt. Malvasia has this salinity in spades, plus something spicy going on. The unique Istriana clone we share with Croatia and Slovenia has been here for centuries and has developed a deep bond with the soil."

The Venica Malvasia always shows a spicy sensation in the nose and a peppery quality on the palate. It has an earthy, almost shell-like quality, deliciously integrated with white pepper. Like the Friulano, it pairs well with prosciutto crudo, but even better with guanciale or speck. It's also great with fish roe. It's possible that Malvasia Istriana is hurt by its confusing name. Neither very popular nor in high demand, it needs the best sites to achieve great results where other grapes can be average, so in a way it's a more challenging grape. Challenging, yes. But due to its vibrant acidity, it feels like drinking liquid electricity.

One producer of note of Malvasia Istriana is Isadoro Princic, known as Doro Princic, in the town of Pradis, which is all of ten homes outside of Cormons in the Collio. I prefer to recommend producers whose wine you can enjoy in the United States, but Doro ships very little of his Malvasia to the States. He does ship his Pinot Bianco, Sauvignon Blanc, and Friulano, and they are all delicious, but he is known locally as the greatest producer of Malvasia.

His Malvasia is the textbook expression of the grape: rich and medium-bodied, with flavors of orange blossoms and citrus flowers, great salty minerality, and not a whiff of oak. It's highly drinkable. Selfishly, I hope all of you petition Doro's importer, Winebow, to bring in more of his Malvasia (many importers just aren't familiar with it, which is why it gets overlooked). We have been lucky over the years to get a few cases at Frasca, and it is one of the most exhilarating things to introduce to our guests. (I have never in all my years had a Malvasia sent back.)

Today, the winery is run by Doro's dedicated son, Sandro Princic and Sandro's lovely wife, Maria Grazia. Sandro is a man with a huge, walrus-like moustache and the ability to eat prosciutto and drink Friulano, Pinot Bianco, and Malvasia alongside the best of them. For years now, when I land in Friuli, I drive straight to the seaside town of Grado to have this wine at Tavernetta all'Androna.

If you happen to book a visit with Sandro, do not book anything else that day. I once shared four magnums with him and Lachlan, and then . . . who knows what happened? Trying to go glass for glass with Sandro is impossible unless you're well-trained. And I consider myself a professional.

This is the reservation you want, even though the winery is not technically a restaurant. One rainy day, Mitja Sirk, our writer Meredith Erickson, photographer William Hereford, and I had the best frittata of our lives made by Maria. Historically, I love Friulano with eggs, but when Sandro poured his 2016 Pinot Bianco, he converted me. It was ripe and, although it topped 14 percent alcohol, had dangerous drinkability. I knew I wanted another glass, but I also knew I had more work to do. Jŏsko Sirk lovingly jokes that guests who have made a dinner reservation at La Subida following a tasting appointment at Princic usually arrive at La Subida completely trashed and very full. (Michele, the sommelier at La Subida, where we usually stay, told us once that a new bottle recycler in town thought Doro Princic was an osteria because of the number of bottles of aromatic white wine he and his friends go through on a regular basis.)

VERDUZZO

This varietal is a singular Friuliano grape. Yes, it can be found in the Veneto, but it's really anchored in Friuli. It can be seen as dry or off-dry. Mostly, we think of it for sweet wine production. Up around the Colli Orientali, it's mostly found in an area near the town of Nimis Ramandolo. I do think it's somewhat ridiculous that the first DOCG was made with this grape. I don't think it has the pedigree for it; almost like it was pay to play. It's not as iconic as the whites of the Collio or Colli Orientali. This varietal, with its thick skin, lends itself to hanging on the vine way past the normal time of harvest, and, like Picolit (see following), makes a sweet wine without botrytis, the "noble rot" that attacks the grape and drains it of its fluids, resulting in a nectar of sweetness.

La Roncaia
Near Cergneu di Nimis, Udine
Colli Orientali

Produced by Marco Fantinel, the Verduzzo of La Roncaia is the best in the region as of late. La Roncaia grows Verduzzo in the coolest northern sites of the Colli Orientali; specifically, in the cold isolated valley near Nimis. It is an unctuous sweet wine—never too intense—that goes down smoothly with a nice piece of gubana (see page 178). It's never going to age as well as Sauternes (the "sweet wine" benchmark) because it's not based on botrytis. It's really a good mid-aging wine. The structure of the Verduzzo grape is very similar to Ribolla Gialla, which is to say, the grape relies on its thick skin to stay late on the vine. Weird Technique Alert: Traditionally, instead of just drying the grapes on the vine, workers cut branches from the vine but leave the grapes on the branches to dry in the sun. The alcohol is high, but the residual sugar is never above 60 grams. In the 1800s, Verduzzo was the third-most-popular white wine in Friuli, and I would love to see it make a comeback, especially the more dry Verduzzos being made by producers such as Fernando and Mario Zanusso at I Clivi.

PICOLIT

Picolit could be the most noble grape you've never heard of. Farmers often abhor Picolit, as many of the grapes "abort" from growing fully (or at all) and ultimately leave little juice to harvest. The grapes that *do* survive, however, are known for their ability to hang late in the year and air-dry on the vine, resulting in unctuous, incredible sweet wine. Essentially, those grapes that do stick around, well, they make it worth your while. With a deep golden hue, Picolit is Friuli's version of France's Sauternes; it is equally delicious served with foie gras.

Some producers in the Collio and Colli Orientali use it as a blending grape for dry wines. Bastianich Tokai Plus (a super-big style of white wine) has a bit of Picolit in it, for example.

I assume they use this because of its perfumed aromatics. The practice seems counterintuitive, to use such a difficult grape that's so hard to grow to blend into your dry whites with *other* grapes, but some producers do it. Livio Felluga is one winery that does not blend the grape.

Livio Felluga
Rosazzo
Colli Orientali

A shining example of good location is on the hill of Rossazo, where the Felluga family grows single-vineyard Picolit on a little sunny bit of slope. While many know the Felluga family from their age-worthy whites, such as Terre Alte and Abbazia di Rosazzo, fewer people are familiar with the power and importance of their Picolit. It is to me one of the best examples of sweet wine in Friuli Venezia Giulia.

The flavor can be rich and unctuous with peach, apricot, and ripe apple as well as notes of Meyer lemon. Unfortunately, little of it is made, and so not much gets into the hands of international wine buyers. When compared to other sweet

Ten Classic Pairings of Friuli

Here's a cheat sheet of our top-ten classic food and wine pairings of the region.

1. Prosciutto di San Daniele with Friulano

One of the best parts of a day in Friuli includes a plate of prosciutto di San Daniele with a glass of Friulano. A good place to go is Enoteca di Cormòns, where you can taste D'Osvaldo ham—the "grand cru" of prosciutto—by the slice, it melts in the mouth (www.dosvaldo.it).

2. Frico Caldo (page 70) with Tocai Friulano

A trip to FVG would be incomplete without frico (fried Montasio cheese) paired with some of the Tocai/Friulano blends. We suggest trying multiple osterie (such as Al Cappello and Al Vecchio Stallo) on a stroll through Udine.

3. White Spring Asparagus (see page 85) with Sauvignon Blanc

If you are traveling to FVG in the spring, try the white asparagus with a glass of Sauvignon Blanc at Valter Scarbolo's La Frasca in Pavia di Udine or Al Grop in Tavagnacco. Both of these restaurants focus entire menus around the asparagus each spring.

4. Smoked Ricotta (see page 219) with Tocai Friulano

An intensely smoky ricotta can be cut only by its ally, a glass of Friulano.

5. Zoff Cheese with Vie di Romans Sauvignon Blanc

In Cormons, there is a fantastic *latteria* (dairy) called Zoff. Buy 225 grams of their cheese and chase it with this wine.

6. Radicchio with Ribolla Gialla

Try the radicchio at Trattoria Al Parco in Buttrio paired with a Ribolla Gialla. FVG is known for having a number of varieties of radicchio that we don't ever see in the United States. Our favorite is the rare Rosa di Gorizia.

7. Pesce Crudo with Malvasia Istriana

Our first stop after landing in FVG is to enjoy a bottle of Malvasia Istriana paired with whole branzino (see page 169), risotto marinara (see page 159), or boreto alla graisana (see page 144) at Tavernetta all'Androna in Grado, where Allan Tarlao takes good care of us. If you can't make it to Grado, try Vitello d'Oro Ristorante in Udine with Max and Gianluca Sabinot, Le Dune in Mariano del Friuli, or Ristorante Al Bagatto in Trieste (see "Our Friuli Address Book," page 252).

8. Charcuterie and Vitovska

Vodopivec or Edi Kante's Vitovska is a winner with any charcuterie and cheese plate.

9. Grilled Meat and Schiopettino

We suggest enjoying a nice Schiopettino with grilled meat at Trattoria Da Toso in Trecisimo or Agriturismo La Planina in Prepotto.

10. Roasted Veal Shank with Macerated Ribolla Gialla

La Subida is a must-visit for this combination, but if you can't make it to Cormons, these wines are not difficult to find, and now neither is the recipe (see page 121).

wines from around the world, Felluga Picolit is competitively priced. It would hold its own against a noted French Sauterne or a Tocai from Hungary. Really, it's one of the great finds in Friuli.

RIBOLLA GIALLA

You cannot talk about Friuli without mentioning Slovenia. The country is that close to the region, and no varietal exemplifies this geographic proximity more than Ribolla Gialla. And Ribolla Gialla is fascinating.

In many parts of Friuli, this varietal is high in acidity and crispness, and low in aromatics. As you creep toward Slovenia and hit towns such as Oslavia and San Floriano del Collio, Ribolla picks up more power. As you cross into Slovenia and enter towns such as Brda, it reaches its greatest heights. This is a grape that needs stress, and the best stress for it is on a sloped vineyard placed only at the top part of the hill so the vines can't be super-productive. If planted on the easier flatlands, the wine becomes watery and much less interesting.

The fence that divides Italy from Slovenia was constructed in 1954. The actual wine region has straddled these two places for hundreds of years. It is really only one wine region with two names: Collio and Brda. The mystical hilltop village of Oslavia, just north of Gorizia, is where Ribolla is taken most seriously. On a series of steep hills right on the border with Slovenia, a group of quiet, hardworking families all focus on this varietal with the utmost intent. Sure, they plant other varietals, but Ribolla is their prized possession because of its natural, beautiful expression of the land. The Friulano varietal needs a touch less rocky soil, and a lower elevation, which is maybe why the rest of the region champions Friulano, but Ribolla works so well in FVG.

Ribolla Gialla can either be unmacerated or macerated, meaning it can be an "orange" wine (see "Vini Macerati," page 40) that's had skin contact, a process that had its renaissance in the late 1990s and has become fashionable in the last ten years. It's no coincidence that the three pillars of maceration—Radikon, Gravner, and La Castellada (all following)—are neighbors. Oslavia is the maceration center of the universe and macerated wines come from the brain trust of those three families. They made the jump together: Radikon in wood, Gravner in amphora, and La Castellada with a more Burgundian touch (meaning French barrique with a certain amount of lee stirring like you would see with white Burgundy). Quite frankly, it took me a while to get my head around these wines at first. I had long enjoyed non-macerated, or traditionally made, wines from all of these producers. Unmacerated, Ribolla is good with light fish, salads, or a piece of prosciutto. I suggest drinking the macerated wines from producers Graver or Radikon with veal shank because of the tannins and dry extract. I also love it with an omakase menu instead of pairing with a red wine!

Wine Collector Alert

I'm also starting to see some sparkling wines made from Ribolla Gialla, including Buzzinelli, a producer very near to La Subida.

Radikon
Near Oslavia, Gorizia
Collio Goriziano

We first took the Frasca staff to Radikon in 2005, and my wife, Danette, and I have been going since 2003. The Radikon family helped usher all of us into the world of macerated wines. They were some of the first people to work with orange wines. Stanko and Suzana and their son, Saša (pictured at left), ran their steep five-hectare estate with minimal assistance during harvest. It does help that Saša is built like a football player, each finger the size of a sausage link. He will hammer a fence post on a January day using only a well-worn pair of boots and his bare hands. He will also tell you that there were times they got it wrong, but now they have a head start on other producers, having been through twenty vintages of this style of wine. When I visited with Lachlan and Frasca sommelier Carlin Karr in 2013, the youngest barrel in their winery was seventeen years old.

Radikon is also synonymous with natural wine. Since 2002, they've used zero sulfur. Of the original macerated producers, Stanko and Saša had experimented with different macerated times each and every year, tinkering with what they feel is best. The Ribolla grape in most hands, especially on the less-steep vineyards in Friuli, is a light-bodied, high-acid, and low-aromatic white grape. Perfect for an aperitivo, almost synonymous with a sparkling wine. Right?

No. Radikon could not be more different. Radikon's Ribolla Gialla is full bodied and with actual tannins from long skin maceration. It is also quite aromatic with the smell of candied peach, white cherries, and bergamot orange. The nose of the wine is far fresher than the dark amber color lets on. These wines can age at a glacial pace for a white wine. For instance, while writing this in the summer of 2019, we opened a 2009 Radikon Ribolla Gialla and it was extremely fresh and youthful.

Stanko passed away in 2016. He was a beautiful man, admired by everyone in the wine world. He had the conviction of his ways but was very far from a dictator of dogma. He was open to all views. I was fortunate to go to his birthday celebration the year after he passed. No restaurants of repute were open in Friuli or Slovenia on that day. Winemakers from all over Italy flew in. I know the winery is in good hands with Saša. And, thank God, those hands are enormous.

Gravner
Near Oslavia, Gorizia
Collio Goriziano

It's very hard to fully explain Jŏsko Gravner (pictured on page 41), which is why you should try to get an appointment with this shy, reticent man who is so passionate about his wines. The first time I had such an appointment, he tried to cancel. My Italian wasn't so good at the time, so I asked my Abruzzese wife, Danette, to tell him how excited we were to be there. Her cajoling worked, and he opened the door and his cellar for us. We proceeded to have a four-hour visit, as he shared with us every strength and weakness he had discovered about his newfound philosophy of maceration.

Vini Macerati

Usually white wines are pulled off their skins immediately, or put under a gentle press. Vini Macerati is made by macerating the skins for a longer period of time. Some producers are known to leave the wines on their skins for up to six months. To put this into perspective, a traditional Barolo producer might macerate Nebbiolo for twenty-one days, which is considered a long time. Vini Macerati is macerated on its skins, usually without the use of sulfur, to produce a white wine that can look heavily oxidized; unfortunately, some of the wines can taste that way. But others beguile with a freshness of apricot and stone fruits. It's a mystical experience, because the wines can taste fresh but have a dark color due to the maceration. Let's also remember not all macerated wines will turn up orange. One such is Paolo Vodopivec's Vitosvka, which can be bright and translucent in color, even though it's been macerated for a long time. So, we shouldn't call *all* macerated wines "orange wines."

I first tasted a macerated wine in 2000, when the 1996 wines were released in the United States. At the time, I was tasked with turning the French Laundry wine list from California-focused to global. I thought by bringing in Gravner white from Friuli, I would show Napa winemakers an example of a powerful, oak-aged, full-bodied white *not* from California. Well, you can imagine my surprise when I opened the first bottles of macerated wines and saw the orange color. I thought they would be full-bodied, textural whites, but after one sip I had no idea what I was tasting. No one knew what to do with these wines. I thought Thomas Keller and his partner Laura Cunningham were going to kill me. The only advantage I had was that I was in the Napa Valley, and I knew George Vare of Luna Vineyards, who turned out to be more fanatical about Friuli wine than I was; he and his winemaker John Kongsgaard had already been to Oslavia the year before and had seen orange wines coming. And so, I got on the phone with him immediately to help me understand what I had in my hand.

Let's just say the first bottles I poured at the French Laundry were met with resistance. And I don't think I even fully grasped what these wines were *entirely* until a 2003 pilgrimage to visit these producers with Lachlan, Danette, and Nate Ready (now one of the most interesting minds in the wine world and a great winemaker at Hiyu Wine Farm in Oregon, but back then, our wild-eyed sommelier at Frasca). These wines have been around for close to twenty years, and now you see orange wines made everywhere, from Napa, Sonoma, France, and Tuscany to Croatia, Slovenia, and beyond. But back then, Vini Macerati was like a bright orange UFO landing in the middle of Napa Valley.

Many sommeliers ask me why we don't have more Vini Macerati on the Frasca wine list. The truth is, while the trend has spread all over the world, Vini Macerati is a pretty small percentage of the wine that is produced and consumed in Friuli Venezia Giulia. FVG macerated wines have a very big megaphone that might lead some people to think that Friuli is all macerated wines, when in reality, most of the great macerated producers are in Oslavia and the Carso. And that's what makes Friulano culture so dynamic.

Jŏsko Gravner is an iconoclastic winemaker. In the late 1960s, he took over the cellar from his father, and he bottled his first wines in 1973. In the early 1980s, he started working with *barriques* (large barrels that last for fifty years or more and don't impart flavor to the wine), and in 1997, he tried his first amphora. In the early 1990s, he was a champion of unoaked wines and then richer, oaky whites. While they're almost all gone now, these early wines were special. In 2019, I got to drink one of his older Sauvignon Blancs and it was amazing; it still had a greenish, fresh hue. In the late 1990s, he fell in love with macerated wines. As of 2005, all of his wines are completely fermented in amphorae sunk into the ground.

Jŏsko will tell you that he lost his motivation to continue making wine in the traditional style after a trip to California and Burgundy made him realize that all international wines are very similar in a way. After another trip, to the country of Georgia, he was inspired to try the macerated style, like his neighbors at Radikon were doing. Two years after that, he started macerating his wines for a long time in amphorae, then aging them in large *botti* (casks). Every big change is very personal. But once the idea was planted, and he was brave enough to move forward fully, his philosophy became about technique and method. Even Jŏsko himself didn't expect the incredible richness coming from the skins. It is a flavor he described to us as "energy transmitting." By preserving the stems and skins, he felt he was getting much closer to the source, that the less you manipulate the grapes, the higher the quality of the wine.

Ribolla Gialla has been growing for more than a thousand years in this area. If you have the climate, the weather, and the right moment, it's as easy to make as lemonade. Gravner's recipe for a great vintage in Oslavia is a dry May and a very dry September and October. In Jŏsko's mind, people are overly focused on sugar. He states, "Just because you're seventeen, doesn't mean you're an adult." What he's saying is that too many people base ripening and harvest on math and not feel. The focus on math is completely counterintuitive to Gravner's philosophy of winemaking.

Gravner's wines are amazing and worthy of aging. It's not uncommon to drink one of his Ribolla Giallas with ten years on it. Sure, they look old because of the color, but the aromatics—stone fruits such as peach and apricot—are always pristine, fresh, and free of flaws. This Ribolla Gialla is one of the eight best glasses of wine of my career.

Sidenote: Winemaker Damijan Podversic, protégé of Jŏsko Gravner with his own style and deft hand, makes Ribolla Gialla in a detailed and vibrant expression, and, as Lachlan says, these wines really let the terroir speak for itself. These wines are rich but not heavy and, similar to Gravner's, do well with quite a bit of age on them. Damijan found a small abandoned plot in the Collio Goriziano, and ignored the common attitude that it is too difficult to work the steepness of this land. When we visited one January, he was rebuilding terraces and his own concrete cellar, a structure fitting for any (organic) Bond villain, atop a hill with views of Oslavia.

La Castellada
Near Oslavia, Gorizia
Collio Goriziano

Nicoló Bensa and his son, Stefano, make powerful, wood-aged macerated wines with a lot of bâtonnage and concentration. I'm always amazed that even for all their power and heft, the wines still have creeping acidity. Like Saša Radikon, Stefano is taking over winemaking operations from his father. I would say that La Castellada makes the most approachable of the macerated wines; tasting their wines is the best way to baby-step into the world of Vini Macerati.

La Castellada labels have two colors on the trim to indicate the amount of time of skin maceration. The orange trim is longer maceration, about two months. Green trim is short maceration, about four days. The green-trim wines, especially Bianco della Castellada, is the gateway wine to macerated wines. Sauvignon Blanc brings an exotic citrus blossom characteristic to the wine, which is captivating. The *élevage* (time between fermentation and bottling) in oak gives these wines finesse that begs for food. It's a powerful, rich white with acid and structure, and can age for twenty-plus years.

I still remember drinking a 2003, which was an incredibly hot vintage (weather-wise), and thinking "this will be dead," only to be surprised by its freshness and liveliness (albeit with a funny hue), even ten years later. It's amazing how these wines are full-bodied and hefty, but don't lose drinkability. On a staff trip in 2008, one of our head waiters, Scott "Scooter" Hagen, was so enthralled tasting the wine that he had to give himself a time-out and take a break in the van. In the previous hour and a half of tasting through the barrels, he had forgotten to spit, and drank the equivalent of three bottles of wine. It was that enchanting.

These are the sexiest of the macerated wines from Oslavia, like a wine whose parents sent it to finishing school. You can serve these with a meal among great bottles of Champagne, white Burgundy, Barolo, and Hermitage, and they will not be out of place.

Tasting Blind

Blind tasting is a hot topic, one that people argue over constantly. In my opinion, wine should be about discovery and learning. To become a master sommelier, you have to pass blind tastings, and though I passed my exam in 2004, I still blind-taste often. As I was writing this paragraph, I stepped out for a moment and was handed a glass of red that I took to be a 2006 Barolo. Wrong. It was a (very tannic) 2009 Sottimano Barbaresco. Blind tasting can be hard on the ego, but it's great for discovery.

As someone who has spent more than fifteen years taking his staff to Friuli, one of the regions that helped to start the natural wine movement, I can confidently say that I love to try *all* wines, from all parts of the world, whether natural or conventional. I like to taste without pretense or hearing a charming backstory—it's amazing how much broader your drinking becomes under such conditions. Wines you never would have conceived of become your biggest loves, and wines you were theoretically prepared to spend your next paycheck on may disappoint you entirely.

It goes without saying that tasting blind takes practice—or what people call work. But I don't think working on a craft is a bad thing.

Ponca at Damijan Podversic's cellar in Collio

The Red Wine Grapes of FVG

I will never be able to play great basketball. I don't have height, wingspan, or agility on my side. But I have other genetic traits that play to my benefit, like being able to sleep anywhere or to polish a rack of wineglasses in less than three minutes. Wine regions, with their strengths and weaknesses, are the same way. As a matter of fact, there are very few regions that make world-class red *and* white wines. Friuli comes the closest with world-class white wines, the ability to make sweet wines, and really, really delicious, regionally specific cool-climate reds.

Friuli is home to indigenous red varietals such as Schioppettino, Refosco, and Pignolo but also international varietals such as Merlot, Cabernet Sauvignon, and Cabernet Franc. These wines are delicious, dynamic, and versatile. People have always consumed lots of red wine in Friuli, and its reds have flourished locally since Napoleonic days—though their style hasn't always been on trend. As the world falls more in love with cold-climate wines and the fresh reds of the Loire, Friuli reds are set to enter the world stage.

Don't be worried if you haven't heard of Terrano, Schioppettino, and so on. We're here to walk you through it, and I will do my best to associate these with wines you're familiar with, but remember that these are all indigenous grapes of Friuli.

SCHIOPPETTINO, AKA RIBOLLA NERA (BLACK RIBOLLA)

What an intellectually stimulating grape! So many things about Schioppettino don't make sense. Why does this red do better in cold or wet vintages, and why does it live and originate in such a weird town?

Schioppettino is probably a native of the village of Cialla, which is one of the coolest sites in the Colli Orientali. You can find these vines all over the Colli Orientali, but usually only on the cooler parcels. It's an aromatic varietal that will lure those who love the aromatic Cab Francs of the Loire, or the narrow-shouldered, peppery northern Rhônes. It's a medium- to full-bodied red, but like an Italian greyhound, there is a singular sleekness to it.

Historically, this grape shares some of the same patterns as Pignolo (see page 46). After World War II, it fell into decline and was almost extinct. But it had been documented in the town of Prepotto, dating as far back as the 1280s. Before phylloxera, Friuli had between two hundred and four hundred biotypes of the varietal. In the 1970s, the Rapuzzi family bought a vineyard in the Cialla area. They waved the flag of Schioppettino and got the little hamlet of Cialla its own DOC. No family is more connected to this varietal; they embrace the grape with a rustic winemaking style that fits Schioppettino so well. If you happen to find a Cialla with age on it, go for it! On one of our visits to Friuli, we drank a 1992 vintage with Pierpaolo Rapuzzi, and it was fantastic.

After my good friend Raj Parr, one of the world's greatest wine minds, tasted a Schioppettino di Petrussa 2014, he tried to buy whatever bottles I had left in the cellar. Why did Raj love this wine so much? It's a classic study in Schioppettino, and 2014 was the coldest vintage in eighty-five years. Many of us think a great red wine needs heat—but think again! This is what many of us love about the Rhône. Schioppettino is intriguing, complex without being bombastic. If you met someone with those traits, wouldn't you want to get to know them better? It reminds me of a cool-climate Syrah—it pulls you in and makes you fall in love with it.

Ronchi di Cialla
Near Cialla di Prepotto, Udine
Colli Orientali

Paulo Rapuzzi (pictured at left) and his wife, Dina, have been on a journey to plant not just Schioppettino but other local indigenous grapes as well. Theirs is what you might call a forty-year "overnight success" story. It's ironic that they've been duking it out since the 1970s and only now are the masses catching on, but as a result, we're seeing a renaissance of these wines. Proving the case, when we visited the Rapuzzis to meet with their son Pierpaolo (whose brother, Ivan, is also in the business), our photographer William Hereford, usually quiet on wine visits, chirped in, "This is the everyday wine that I buy from my wine guy in Brooklyn!" (Fun Fact: When not pruning the already niche vines of Schioppettino, the Rapuzzi brothers can be found behind microscopes studying long-horned beetles as they are both well-known entomologists!)

It's not only young wine buyers from London, Rome, and New York who are interested in this grape, though. International winemakers are also hunting it down. For those of you who haven't tried it, it has aromatics of peppered meats, peppercorn, tart cranberry, and tart black fruits. It's wonderful with sausages, grilled meats, and even a hamburger!

Another producer who makes *delicious* Schioppettino is Lorenzo Mocchiutti at Vignai da Duline (see page 50). Lorenzo's Schioppettino tends to be a little bit rounder and fuller than that made at Ronchi di Cialla. Its site in Buttrio might be one of the southernmost spots for this wine.

PIGNOLO

Talk about a varietal that almost went the way of the dodo bird! The Pignolo grape was thought to be extinct when, in the early 1970s, it was found nestled in the back of a garden at the Abbazia di Rosazzo (it was customary for monasteries to keep exemplars of the local flora on their property). So right there, on the hill of Rosazzo, Pignoli vines were revived. Now we can enjoy Pignolo from a number of producers. While there aren't a lot of them (only about twenty hectares of Pignolo are planted in all of Italy), the ones who have been working with it—wonderful producers from Le Vigne di Zamò to Dario Ermacora—are doing a great job.

Pignolo is a fussy varietal not favored by many winemakers because it's difficult to work with, having low yields, big tannins, and high acidity. At its best, it reminds me of a powerful Cabernet combined with the acidity of a Nebbiolo. It's dark in color and needs long aging in oak. The wine itself can age for years. The great thing about Pignolo, though, is you can make it direct and honest without needing new French oak, or you can make it in a more international style with toasty new

wood. In all cases, it's a pleasure to drink. What do you want to eat with this? Great game, rabbit, and roast pork. This is the perfect red wine for meats that are grilled off the *fogolar*, the classic indoor freestanding grilling hearth famous in Friuli.

Wine Collector Alert

This osterie list is incredible and you can go off-piste, or off the beaten path. It's a Frasca team favorite as the list is vast with Italian bottles that have a bit of age on them.

Ronco delle Betulle
Near Rosazzo, Udine
Colli Orientali

Giovanni Battista Adami founded Ronco delle Betulle in 1967 on the slopes of the hill of Rosazzo in the Colli Orientali. Though Giovanni started the estate, the power behind this great winery today lies with the mother-son duo of Ivana Adami and Simone Secchi. They make a great team, with Ivana running the winery and Simone overseeing the logistics and day-to-day business. Ivana's winemaking hand allows for powerful wines with great elegance and finesse, like their Pignolo. Ronco delle Betulle Pignolo is a dark, full-bodied, meaty red wine that takes many years to age. It is almost like a glacier in how slowly it evolves. But once it starts to open up, it gives great aromatics of leather, forest floor, and dark fruits.

It's not uncommon for me and some friends to show up to the estate thinking we'll just have a little glass of Friulano from the large barrels, only to have Ivana and Simone pull together a couple of picnic tables and set up a full meal in a minute, with housemade salami, frico, and maybe even a pasta course with ragù.

REFOSCO, AKA REFOSCO DAL PEDUNCOLO ROSSO

Refosco has the peppery spice that Rhône fans adore, but it comes with the kind of acidity you find in wines from cold-climate, elevated mountain regions. For example, for many years, people thought Refosco was related to the varietal Mondeuse (a cool-climate red from the Savoie in the French Alps). I can see the reason for the confusion because of the mountain tie-in. In a region that is so well-known for whites, here is a great red that has enough heartiness for winter dishes (it's perfect with potato and herb cjalsòns, see page 225), but has a brightness that you can enjoy in the summer with a simple grilled pork tenderloin.

I've found a lot of pleasure from drinking less-expensive Refosco, planted on lighter soil, from the Grave region, but when I think of it at its highest highs, I think of Duline (see following) or Miani (see page 19). *Peduncolo rosso* means "red stalk"; the stalks of this varietal are reddish violet, much like the color of the wine in the glass. For those who find Friuli white wines too "hot" (wine speak for "too high in alcohol"), a slightly chilled Refosco is the perfect choice.

Vignai da Duline
Near San Giovanni al Natisone, Udine
Colli Orientali

There are two producers who make vanguard-style Refosco wines: Lorenzo Mocchiutti at Duline, and Enzo Pontoni at Miani. Lorenzo and his wife, Federica Magrini (pictured at left), who run Vignai da Duline on a beautiful slope in the Collio, met in the 1980s when they were both vegan squatters and Lorenzo was in a punk band called Argy Bargie. In the late 1990s, they inherited a few hectares of vines from Lorenzo's grandfather, vineyards that for the most part had been neglected for decades and were planted primarily with old vines of local grape varieties such as Malvasia Istriana, Tocai Fruilano, Schioppettino, and Refosco.

Since then, they have been hard at work with those same varietals, using a respectful, holistic approach to vineyard management that is summed up in their philosophy of "no trimming the shoots" and "no herbicides." Inspired by the philosophy and teachings of Masanobu Fukuoka and his book *One Straw Revolution*, Lorenzo and Federica use intuition and experimentation to make their wines. Today, their vineyards cover seven hectares divided between hillsides and flatlands, including Ronco Pitotti, one of the oldest hillside vineyards in Friuli, with vines dating back to the 1920s. Walking here is a peaceful experience. Among the vines are wildflowers, local flora, and a lot of insects, all working in harmony. Instead of using herbicides, they plant a type of alfalfa, *erba medica*, that suppresses weeds and acts as a natural fertilizer when cut.

A few years ago, famous American wine importer Kermit Lynch was having lunch at our favorite Venetian restaurant, Osteria alle Testiere. He was poured a glass of one of Duline's wines and was thrilled by what he tasted. Kermit then wrote Lorenzo and Frederica an old-school letter, saying how honored he would be to import their wines into the United States. Lorenzo and Frederica kept the letter and proudly showed it to me during their visit. What a perfect fit: Kermit is a Berkeley, California, icon, and Lorenzo and Federica embody the mores of free-thinking Berkeley in their winemaking practice.

These wines really capture terroir, regardless of the varietal, but the Refosco is particularly worthy. This is a wine that sings with potato gnocchi, rabbit ragù, or polenta with some braised short ribs. If you're Sangiovese fan, you might like the brisk "cut-ness" (a slight tart hit) of this Refosco.

TERRANO

There are a few different clones of Refosco, and one of them is Terrano. The Carso—a wild, almost uninhabitable, place for grapes—most likely forced mutation of the clone. Terrano is nothing like its cousin Refosco. It's a wine that's naturally tart and tangy. Even when it's perfectly ripe and you think you will taste a wine that has some cuddle to it, a bit of roundness, it surprises you with cut and precision. There is a rumor that the doctors of Trieste once prescribed this to women with anemia because of its high iron content.

Edi Kante
Near Prepotto, Trieste
Carso

Edi Kante, a producer known for making great Carso-based white wines, from Vitovska to Chardonnay to Sauvignon Blanc, makes one of the best Terranos in the Carso. These wines taste like nothing else in the region, and perhaps that's because these vines are planted at higher than 820 meters in elevation, making them practically Alpine. They're bright, with lively acidity and low tannins but full of structure from the acidity. While grape varietals such as Barbera have a high acidity, they have more of a cushion of fruit than Terrano. It is a red wine that does well with a slight chill on it.

TAZZELENGHE

This grape's name translates to "tongue-cutter," likely because of its tannins and high acidity. Anyone who is working with Tazzelenghe is committed, simply because it is not that fashionable or easy to sell. That's partly because a thousand years ago, ripeness was a harder thing to come by (due to temperatures), and the wine fell out of fashion. But now, through modern viticulture and the unfortunate effects climate change, these wines have higher ripeness levels than in the past. And this might just be the little nudge it needs to keep the wine 100 percent authentic. Aromatically complex with a lot of dark fruit, this wine can be enjoyed with anything wildly decadent, rich, or fatty.

La Viarte
Near Venćo, Udine
Colli Orientali

I wish there were more people experimenting with this grape, but there are only a few producers making Tazzelenghe. Modern-day viticulture might give this cool-climate red varietal another chance at having more application at the table. The best current example of this grape is in the hands of La Viarte vineyard in the Colli Orientali. It was planted in 1983 by the Ceschin family, whose son, Giulio, now runs the winery with his wife, Federica. He and business partner, Alberto Piovam, expanded La Viarte to forty-one hectares, including seventeen hectares of forest that they conserve to maintain the area's ecological balance. They continue to focus on local heirloom varieties, such as Friulano, Schioppettino, Tazzelenghe, and Verduzzo. Their Tazzelenghe is tannic with high acidity that is rough in its youth but mellows with age.

Significant Moments in FVG Wine History (1950s–present day)

1950s: Livio Felluga buys vineyards in Friuli and begins bottling wine, establishing recently farmed FVG as a winemaking region after the end of World War II.

1960s: Mario Schiopetto goes into wine production and, in 1965, brings out the first bottle of Tocai, ushering in a new era of modern white winemaking in Italy.

1970s: The rise of single-varietal grappa coincides with the rise of the Italian socialist movement.

1980s: Enter Jösko Gravner, who begins barreling whites in the Burgundian style instead of fermenting them in stainless-steel tanks as had been the norm. Nicola Manferrari of Borgo del Tiglio also makes wine in the Burgundy style.

1990s: Maceration and what some call the Orange Wine era begins. Producers are also trying to make wines with oak and extraction as was happening in California and parts of France.

2000s: The *Tre Bicchieri* ("three glasses") guidebook for Italophiles in the United States in the late 1990s and early 2000s is where it is at. The guidebook tells somms and restaurateurs who is doing great work and producing interesting wines in Italy; almost like a speculation guide for importers. During this period, the Venica family is producing many Ronco delle Mele Sauvignon Blanc bottles and much attention is brought to the region of Friuli, and to the Sauvignon Blanc varietal. (Though they are not as important as they once were, the *Tre Bicchieri* guidebooks and some awards definitely did a lot for the region during this era.)

2010s: Young winemakers start to produce new wines either as a side hustle from their family business or to just go out on their own. For example, Giampaolo Venica, while working at Venica, works on his own wine. Mitja Sirk, while working at La Subida, makes great Friulano.

Wood and copper vats at Nonino Distillery

In Praise of Firewater: A Note on Grappa

In 1970s Italy, vodka was all the rage—and the world assumed that grappa tasted like gasoline.

Originally, grappa was made by peasants using the pomace (grapes, stems, and sticks left over from the winemaking process; basically, the by-product of the prime material) to create a fortifying liquor for the wintertime. *Mezzadria* (sharecropper living) was the way of life, and grappa was a necessity, not a luxury. Just like the French had marc in Burgundy, the Italians—specifically those in the Veneto, Alto Adige, and Friuli regions—had grappa.

To make grappa, you wait for the August arrival of the pomace from red and white grapes, then distill it in large copper vats (or whatever is available) for three months. The resulting liquid—technically, a neutral brandy—is grappa. Up until the 1960s, grappa producers (who could be almost anyone) could slap a label on a bottle and sell their (somewhat harsh) wares. But in the late 1960s and early 1970s, Giannola and Benito Nonino changed everything.

The Noninos are a Friulano phenomenon. Although the family owned a distillery dating back to the 1890s, it wasn't until the late 1960s that Giannola, being a restless and innovative woman, decided the world needed a refined and sophisticated digestif. "Let's make grappa from the grape!" she said. "Not just using the stems, not just the bits but the skins. And let's not blend the grape skins, but let's do single-varietal grappa too!"

What happened next was a huge investment and risk. The Noninos bought up grand cru vineyards all over Friuli, specifically in the Colli Orientali. Here they planted Picolit, Ribolla Gialla, Fragolino, Schioppettino, and Sauvignon grapes *solely for the purpose of making grappa.*

While the rest of the world was buying pomace, they were purchasing vineyards in the Butrio—in the same neighborhood as producers such as Meroi and Pontoni.

The idea to make single-vineyard grappa did not start with Chardonnay or Pinot Noir. It started with a notoriously difficult grape to grow: Picolit. Farmers don't like to plant it because it has the propensity to abort its grapes midlife, which makes obtaining a healthy yield challenging. But if you do manage to yield enough and then distill it, you're off to the races. If that wasn't enough risk, Gianolla also modeled the bottles for their product on an apothecary-style vial—not the heavy-shouldered grappa bottles of the past—custom-built glass bottles that would look beautiful on a woman's dresser or in a dining room, like a seductive elixir. It did not hurt that the Noninos were close in proximity to the talented glass-blowers of Murano and Venice!

To go a step further, Gianollo contacted the wives of winemakers, asking them to set aside their grape skins. She offered ten times the going rate for those skins in order to incentivize the women to work for themselves and have their own financial independence. The first production was in 1973, and almost the entire inventory went unsold. People were not used to paying high prices for grappa.

Natural Selection: On the Origin of Drinkability

When you open a lot of bottles during a dinner party, what wines are left over at the end? Many times, it seems the well-known, big-score wines are those that remain in glasses and bottles. But the bottle of Schioppettino and that Sauvignon Blanc will have vanished. Why? Friuli wines are more drinkable than wines from other regions. In Friuli, white wines can have weight but not be clumsy, and red wines can be svelte and still completely delicious and intriguing.

But Gianolla showed up at the best events, and the most refined restaurants, with her grappa at the ready. Because of the historically low quality of grappa, the market was open to something new. And soon enough, she won over the world, starting with Italy. The Noninos didn't open the window for high-quality distillation products, they blew out the whole house!

When we visited the distillery on a rainy spring day, we accidentally went to Benito and Gianolla's home first. Gianolla came running out in a bathrobe to greet us, jumped into her sports car, curlers still in her hair, and floored it to the distillery. Here, we were greeted enthusiastically (and that's an understatement) by her three daughters and (many) glass trays of amaro cocktails (see Aperitivo Nonino, facing page). Over three hours, they fed us, poured us (too much) beautiful grappa, and showed us their warehouse, a stunning old airplane hangar with massive copper vats, many with the names of the family's children labeled on the front.

The distillery and their worldwide domination is a testament to their vision. No family has higher standards. Just as they are the standard bearer for grappa, the Nonino amaros are also blue chip. At Frasca Food and Wine, we built a custom grappa and amaro cart. While it contains a mix of producers, it was in full sincerity custom-built for the objects d'art that are the Nonino bottles. And what's truly amazing is that you can taste the varietal character of these grapes even after the distillation process. Today, the company is run by the three trailblazing daughters, Cristina, Antonella, and Elisabetta, who, in keeping with their parents' vision, have made grappa evolve from its humble beginnings to the *Cederina alla regina* (Cinderella of the region).

From left: Elisabetta, Gianolla, Cristina, and Antonella Nonino

APERITIVO NONINO
(Amaro Giannola-Style)

Makes 1 serving

Tastewise this is similar to a *bicicletta* (half parts white wine to Campari), but it calls for grappa and Champagne, so it's less delicate and more full-throttle. The bad news/ good news is that this goes down easy. This was the drink the Nonino family served when we arrived at their home, which was perfect, as it's fittingly high voltage and elegant.

Ice cubes

1 orange slice

1 tablespoon Amaro Nonino Quintessentia

¾ cup Champagne or sparkling wine of your choice

In an aperitivo glass, combine a few ice cubes, the orange slice, and amaro and top up with the Champagne. Serve immediately.

Land

When we talk about the land of Friuli Venezia Giulia, we're referring to the plateau, or the mid-section of the region, that is layered between Carnia to the north and the Adriatic to the south, the Italian Veneto to the west and Slovenia to the east. This—both geographically and structurally in this book—is the real meat and potatoes of Friuli, or in this case, the prosciutto and polenta. This region is also all about the vineyards, which means it's the heartland of the frasca, where locals welcome you into their homes to taste their new wines. If you're going to tour this area, you will want to start the day with Jŏsko Sirk's famous eggs at La Subida. Fried in a cast-iron pan in a *fogolar* (hearth) with a spritz of homemade vinegar, these eggs are a fitting introduction to what lies outside the doorstep of Cormons and greater Friuli.

Sampling prosciutto is another good way to start exploring the region. There are three *prosciuttoficios* (prosciutto manufacturers) that you cannot miss in Friuli: Wolf in Sauris (Carnia), La Casa del Prosciutto ("the home of ham") in San Daniele, and D'Osvaldo in Cormons. It's normal on a weekday morning for there to be a line out the door at D'Osvaldo, as people flock from all over Italy to buy as much of what we call the grand cru of prosciutto as will fit in their Fiats. The prosciutto of San Daniele is a highly regarded rival to the well-known prosciutto di Parma; both are mandated to be made from a pig born in Italy, yet here in FVG, the pigs themselves are responsible for only a fraction of the finished product. It has famously been said that it takes a few simple things to create beautiful charcuterie: a pig, salt, air, and time—and in San Daniele it is no different. The town's position, just down from the Carnic Alps but still on a hill, defines the cured ham's success. Also, in this case, the air currents sweeping down from the Alps and up from the sea make the curing-air magic happen.

This area is also home to most of the frascas of FVG, as it encompasses almost all of the wine regions; the two hillside Denominations of Origin (aka DOCs; Friuli Colli Orientali and Collio Goriziano) and four of the flatland DOCs (Lison-Pramaggiore, Friuli Latisana, Friuli Grave, and Friuli Isonzo). We've spent a lot of time in the vineyard towns of this region, places such as Buttrio, Cialla, Capriva, Gorizia, and, of course, the famous hills of Rosazzo all have little *osterias* (taverns) nestled among the green and rolling vineyards.

In the western part of Friuli, around the beautiful, light, gravelly soil in the Grave wine region, are the towns of Pordenone and Aviano. Aviano may sound familiar to some Americans because a major air force base is located there. No matter what time of year it is, it's always possible to see US Air Force jets working on skills and techniques, flying over the vineyards and racing toward the Alps. Because there is also a locally stationed Italian Air Force base, you may see other acrobatic pilots doing the same skill sets. It's actually quite exciting!

One of our favorite restaurants to visit in western Friuli is La Primula, an establishment that has been family-owned for more than 120 years. It has an incredible, affordable, really well-thought-out wine list; one of which wine dreams are made. Many a time, Giampaolo Venica (see page 23) and I and our spouses have flipped a coin to see who will drive there from Cormons, the winner taking all (the wine, but not the steering wheel).

Our favorite city in Friuli is Udine, where you will find Osteria Al Cappello. We suggest spending a Saturday afternoon at this small, kitschy, and lively wine bar; we love to enjoy the company of winemakers while drinking Miani Friulano (see page 19; unlike the other 99 percent of the world, they always have Miani here) and observing the influx of Austrians who come to shop *Italiano*—the Udinese tailors are legendary—and have lunch. A beautiful chalkboard wall stretches along one side of the restaurant detailing the wines available. Monica Toniut, the restaurant's owner, works hard to produce wonderful, honest osteria food, such as homemade sausage, polenta, and addictive *pizzetas* (small pizzas). It's a great spot to enjoy the Friulano lifestyle while getting a sense of Friulano food and wine in a truly local setting. (In all of Bobby's years as a sommelier, few have ever seen him suffer from a hangover, but on one exceptional trip, he was cured by Monica's lunch. Thank you kindly, Richard Betts.)

In Udine, you will also find the Archeological Museum, the Gallery of Modern Art, the Gallery of Ancient Art, the Drawings and Stamps Gallery, and the Friulian Photography Museum. We visit Friuli four to six times a year, and each time, we flirt with the idea of buying a piazza-facing apartment in culturally rich Udine. As a footnote to Udine, but impressive on its own, about thirty kilometers to the south is the UNESCO heritage city of Palmanova, a fifteenth-century fortress built by the Venetian Republic. It is shaped like a nine-point star and is an FVG landmark.

To the east of Udine is the town of Cividale del Friuli. Set right on the slopes of the eastern hills just south of the Carnic Prealps, this is a cozy village where we often stop for a quick espresso (which they call *una nero*) at Caffè Longobardo, a very busy Friulian meeting place for cyclists about to venture north through the mountains or east to Slovenia. The ride's starting point crosses the famous Devil's Bridge over the river Natisone. The bridge was built in the fifteenth century (and then rebuilt in 1918 after it was bombed during the First World War).

Our next stop is often the town of Cialla, where we are back in the Colli Orientali among the rolling hills; this is where you'll find the Rapuzzi family vineyard Ronchi di Cialla (see page 46). These hills (*ronc*, in Friulano) have singular sun exposure, and many native, or indigenous, Friulian grapes grow here. From Cialla, it is only a fifteen-minute jog to Slovenia, where Western Europe ends and the East begins.

In the pages that follow, you'll find recipes for *contorni* (snacks to go alongside your first glass of wine), pork (in its prosciutto and non-prosciutto forms), and a smattering of game (venison and pheasant), which is reserved for special occasions by most Friulians. This area is also the grain heartland, so polenta looms large here—both dressed up and down.

The ingredients in these recipes are simple, but like all Italian recipes, the meat, grains, and vegetables should be of the highest quality in order to yield the most delicious result. The dishes, like the region itself, are understated. *Blecs* (handmade pasta) and tagliolini, for example, may not appear to be as mouthwatering as they actually are. It's only when you begin to make and taste these recipes that you realize how much more Friuli you need in your life. Trust us.

CONTORNI

In Friuli, *contorni* (literally, "side dishes") can be a welcome snack and an excuse for a glass of Tocai Friulano. Toast with a *tajùt*—a glass of wine offered up with some cheese and ham slices, small bites of seasonal fruit or vegetables, or even a bowl of potato chips and nuts. This is a tradition we live by, and so should you! Whether you're stepping into a century-old café in Trieste, like Antico Caffè San Marco, or invited into a winemaker's home in the Collio, the time is always right for this simple daily Friuli ritual. The key here is simplicity; all you need are a few small plates, bowls, or wood boards to present these nibbles for your guests: figs wrapped in thin slices of guanciale (pictured opposite), zucchini blossoms stuffed with ricotta and then fried, homemade potato chips, and handmade skinny breadsticks (see page 68) wrapped in prosciutto.

Fig and Guanciale
Makes 4 servings

4 fresh figs, halved   8 thin slices guanciale

Wrap each fig half in a slice of guanciale and skewer with a toothpick to secure. We like to roast these in a cast-iron skillet set directly on a bed of smoldering coals for about 5 minutes, turning them once or twice. If an outdoor fireplace is not an option, place them on a baking sheet, cut-side up, under the broiler for 2 to 3 minutes, then flip them over and continue to broil for another minute or so. Keep a close eye on them; the guanciale should become crispy but not burned. Serve immediately.

Stuffed Squash Blossoms
Makes 4 servings

YOU WILL NEED
Piping bag fitted with small plain tip

1 cup fresh ricotta, seasoned with a generous pinch of fine sea salt

8 thin slices pancetta

¼ cup olive oil

8 squash or zucchini blossoms, pistils removed

Transfer the ricotta to a piping bag fitted with a small plain tip. Gently fill each blossom with about 2 tablespoons of the seasoned ricotta, then twist the petals to close. Wrap each stuffed blossom in a slice of pancetta and place seam-side down on a plate.

In a medium frying pan over medium-low heat, warm the olive oil. Place the blossoms in the pan, seam-side down, and cook until the pancetta starts to turn golden brown and caramelize, about 3 minutes. Lower the heat as needed and rotate the blossoms until all sides are golden brown, about 5 minutes more. Serve immediately.

Potato Chips

Makes 4 servings; about 8 cups

YOU WILL NEED
Mandoline
Deep fryer or heavy pot
Deep-frying thermometer

4 medium Yukon gold potatoes	1 rosemary sprig
5 cups canola oil	Fine sea salt
4 fresh sage leaves	

Fill a large bowl with hot tap water.

Using a mandoline or a very sharp knife, slice the potatoes very thinly, approximately ¹⁄₁₆ inch thick, and then transfer to the bowl of hot water. Let the slices soak for up to 30 minutes to release some of their starch. Drain the water and pat the potatoes completely dry with a kitchen towel.

Line a baking sheet with a double layer of paper towels.

In a deep fryer or a heavy pot over medium heat, warm the canola oil until a thermometer registers 300°F. Toss in the sage leaves and rosemary sprig.

Working in batches and using a spider (or your hands if you're a confident deep-fryer), carefully lower one-fourth of the potato slices into the oil. Use the spider to stir the slices frequently, until cooked and golden brown, 3 to 5 minutes. Transfer to the prepared baking sheet and then fry the remaining potato slices, one batch at a time.

Transfer the cooked chips to a platter or bowl, season generously with salt, and let cool. If not serving immediately, store in an airtight container, at room temperature, for up to 12 hours.

GRISSINI

Makes about 60 breadsticks

Grissini clustered next to a charcuterie board with some sliced cheese is a common sight to see upon walking into a winemaker's home. The word *grissini* derives from the Piedmontese word for "little line or row." Although many restaurants in Friuli buy little packages of grissini to serve before or with meals, at Frasca, we make about 1,500 breadsticks per week, year-round. They are light, delicate, and the perfect vehicle for the most delicious of Italian cured hams. We make our favorite snack more Friulian by wrapping each breadstick with very thinly sliced prosciutto San Daniele, and suggest you do the same.

YOU WILL NEED
Manual pasta machine with tagliatelle cutter attachment
Instant-read digital thermometer (optional)

⅔ cup whole milk

1 tablespoon active dry yeast

2 cups bread flour

1 tablespoon sugar

2 tablespoons extra-virgin olive oil, plus more for brushing

1 tablespoon unsalted butter, at room temperature

Fine sea salt

Using a microwave, warm the milk to approximately 104°F (but no hotter than 115°F); it should feel a little warmer than lukewarm. Stir in the yeast and set aside.

In the bowl of a food processor, combine the flour, sugar, olive oil, butter, and 1½ teaspoons salt. Pulse several times until the mixture looks crumbly, then pulse a few more times until dough begins to come together.

Turn the dough and any remaining flour bits onto a clean work surface, gather into a ball, and knead until smooth, 1 to 2 minutes. Grease a mixing bowl with a thin coat of olive oil, place the dough in the bowl, and refrigerate for 1 hour.

Dust a baking sheet or your counter with flour. Slice the dough ½ inch thick. Keep the dough covered while working with one slice at a time.

Flatten the slice a little with the palm of your hand. Roll out the dough in a pasta machine as you would fresh pasta dough (see page 88, steps 2 to 4), but only until the third or fourth setting. Set the sheet of dough aside on the prepared baking sheet or the flour-dusted counter. Repeat the rolling process with the remaining slices of dough.

Preheat the oven to 300°F. Line two baking sheets with parchment paper.

Feed each sheet of dough through the tagliatelle cutter attachment. Use scissors or a sharp knife to cut the strands to your preferred length—we like 10 inches. Arrange the thin strands on the prepared baking sheets; the strands can be very close together but should not be touching. Use a pastry brush to brush the grissini with olive oil, then sprinkle with a liberal amount of salt.

Bake one sheet at a time, rotating at the halfway mark, until golden brown, about 20 minutes. Let cool on the baking sheet. Store in an airtight container, at room temperature, for up to 6 weeks.

FRICO CALDO
(Hot Frico)

Makes 6 to 8 servings

Frico is to Friuli what pizza is to Naples. An essential element in Friulano cuisine, frico was created as a way to use up scraps and bits of rind left over from wheels of Montasio, the cow's milk cheese for which Friuli has become most known. When we are traveling in Friuli and meet someone who finds out we own a Friulano-inspired restaurant, the first question is always, "Do you serve frico?"

There are two types of frico: *caldo* and *croccante* (see facing page). Caldo, the hot version, usually combines potatoes with cheese and onions to produce a sort of ridiculously rich hash brown–like bubble that begins to deflate at your table when cooling, or when unceremoniously popped.

Notes

If you don't have a well-seasoned cast-iron pan, using a large nonstick pan makes the process much easier. We use a 4-inch square cast-iron pan at the restaurant that we simply call the frico pan.

For a garnish, we like a splash of herbed vinaigrette. Combine 1 tablespoon minced fresh flat-leaf parsley or cilantro with a splash of lemon juice and good olive oil, then season with salt and pepper.

YOU WILL NEED

Potato ricer

1¼ pounds russet potatoes	1 teaspoon fine sea salt
4 tablespoons olive oil	¼ teaspoon freshly grated nutmeg
½ cup diced yellow onion	
½ pound Montasio cheese (aged six months or less), grated	Herb vinaigrette (see Note) and/or pomegranate seeds for serving

In a large pot of unsalted water over high heat, boil the potatoes until fork-tender, 30 to 40 minutes depending on the size of the potatoes. Transfer to a plate to cool. When cool enough to handle, peel off the skin. Cut two-thirds of the potatoes into medium dice and transfer to a large bowl. Pass the remaining one-third of the potatoes through a ricer into the same bowl.

In a medium frying pan over medium heat, warm 2 tablespoons of the olive oil. Add the onion and sauté gently until translucent, 7 to 9 minutes.

Add the Montasio, cooked onion, salt, and nutmeg to the potatoes. Gently mix by hand until all the ingredients have been evenly incorporated. (This mixture can be refrigerated for up to 24 hours.)

In a large cast-iron skillet or nonstick frying pan over high heat, warm the remaining 2 tablespoons olive oil until almost smoking. Add the potato mixture and use a spatula to flatten it into a ½-inch-thick, 10-inch-wide cake, rounding and evening out the edges with the spatula.

Turn the heat to medium and cook, without moving or stirring, until a golden-brown crust starts to form along the edges and the underside of the frico, about 5 minutes. Once a nice caramel-colored crust has formed, lay a plate or a large pot lid facedown over the frying pan and flip the frico over. Then slip the frico back into the frying pan, crust-side up, and continue cooking until it is golden in color on the second side, another 5 minutes. Remove from the pan and let rest on a cutting board for 2 minutes.

Once the frico has cooled slightly, cut into the desired number of portions and serve with an herb vinaigrette and/or a sprinkle of pomegranate seeds.

FRICO CROCCANTE
(Frico Pops)

Makes 12 to 15 servings

The first time we saw a frico "pop" was at La Subida. Jŏsko Sirk handed each of us a glass of sparkling Ribolla Gialla from Buzzinelli along with what looked like a lollipop made of crispy fried cheese. Typically, Montasio vecchio, or aged Montasio, can be fried and cooled; it's the kind of thing a hunter would have in a knapsack to munch on. At Frasca, we love it as a playful starter for every guest. These are completely addictive, as well as incredibly easy and fast to make in a microwave oven. We suggest poking the skewers into a rustic boule of bread to serve. These can also be stored in an airtight container, at room temperature, for up to 3 days, but will lose some of their crispiness.

YOU WILL NEED

Twelve to fifteen 4-inch squares parchment paper or a
    small silicone baking mat that fits in your microwave
Twelve to fifteen 4- to 6-inch bamboo skewers
2-inch cookie cutter or ring mold

¼ pound Montasio vecchio
cheese (aged one year or
longer), grated

Lay a square of parchment paper on a small plate. Lay down one bamboo skewer vertically, then lay a 2-inch cookie cutter on top of the skewer—picture the cookie cutter as the lollipop on a stick, that is, the skewer should go halfway inside the ring mold.

Using your fingers, pinch a good amount of cheese into the ring mold, about ⅛ inch high. Use your fingers to gently arrange the cheese strands to even them out, but do not be tempted to pat them down inside the mold. Remove the mold.

Transfer the plate to the microwave and cook for 25 to 30 seconds—this will vary according to the microwave, you may need more time; the cheese will bubble furiously, spread out, and start to color slightly. When you remove the plate from the microwave, the cheese crisps should be more golden yellow than orange or dark brown. Peel off the paper and taste the frico to make sure it is crispy and the color is to your liking, then lay it onto a paper towel. Repeat with a fresh square of parchment on a fresh (cool) plate, using another bamboo skewer, the ring mold, and more cheese. Serve immediately.

Friuli's Polenta, the OG of Polenta

Polenta has been a staple of Friulian cuisine for hundreds of years. In fact, before there was corn in Friuli Venezia Giulia, natives used buckwheat to make polenta (the word *polenta* comes from the Latin for "hulled, peeled barley"). With Columbus's introduction of maize, the story goes that polenta brightened up.

Polenta is a dish that can take on many forms; from soft, warming porridge to crisped batons as a side with a meat-based protein, or as a canvas for cooked greens or mushrooms in the fall. Practically straddling the border with Slovenia in the still-Italian town of Dolegna del Collio is Molino Tuzzi, a mill that's been in the same family since 1895 (and housed in a structure that's been around since the 1400s). For five generations and through two world wars, the mill has milled corn. When times were rough and necessity called for it, the mill sheltered soldiers while simultaneously grinding corn for the entire region of the Collio.

In the 1970s, the business took a more gastronomic turn with a focus on the highest-quality product; starting in the mid-1990s, Tuzzi became the first corn-flour producer in the region to use biodynamic cultivation. Enrico Tuzzi is the current custodian, and the structure is the only artisanal mill in all of Gorizia, Trieste, and the Slovenian territory near the border, supporting hundreds of small Italian and Slovenian farmers, and by extension, ensuring that the indigenous varieties and the agricultural heritage of the Collio not only survives but thrives. One of these varieties is a white corn, farmed in the Veneto and Collio areas, known as *specheote*, which tends to be paired with seafood dishes.

The Tuzzi mill is at the heart of a chain of food producers working to enrich the food history as well as the current story of Friuli. However, Molino Tuzzi products will prove difficult, if not impossible, to find in North America, so we suggest you order polenta (both white and yellow) from Anson Mills, a company in South Carolina committed to milling organic heirloom grains. We use their products at Frasca: fine white polenta (mild and especially good with fish or seafood), fine yellow polenta (classic), and rustic polenta integrale (whole-milled, whole-grain corn grits). Alternatively, look for Bob's Red Mill Organic Polenta Corn Grits at your local supermarket.

Polenta service at La Subida

TOC' IN BRAIDE
("Farm Gravy")

Makes 4 to 6 servings

Often served as an appetizer, toc' in braide is really a way to make the usual and classic polenta, well, *different*. The result is a soft polenta that's been enriched with a cheese fonduta. This particular version was inspired by the late Gianni Cosetti, a Friulian chef known throughout Italy for transforming humble, native ingredients into elegant and luxurious dishes. Many winemakers have fond memories of going to his restaurant, Ristorante Roma, in Tolmezzo (north of Udine) in the 1980s and '90s. Roma was a small restaurant of just eight tables inside an old hotel and, like many other spots in the area, you didn't realize you were in for a major gastronomic experience until the food started coming out of the kitchen. Gianni was the Jeremiah Tower of Italy: elegant, whip-smart, and dangerously fun. He almost singlehandedly brought the cooking of Carnia, and its best ingredients, into the realm of gourmet dining. He died all too soon in 2001.

The great thing about polenta is that it's comfortable and stylish in its own clothes (see "Friuli's Polenta, the OG of Polenta" on page 72). It can be a successful, simple weeknight dish, or it can be fashionable, as Gianni's was, with his addition of seared foie gras. Our recipe doesn't include foie, but it does have the base polenta and Parmesan broth—a no-frills approach, the OG toc' in braide, if you will, that results in an incredibly cheesy-tasting umami bomb.

Notes
The Parmesan brodo must simmer for 5 hours, so plan accordingly.

Prior to cooking, we toast the polenta until it takes on a golden color and has a very strong aroma of perfectly roasted corn. To finish, we pour over a cheese crema with a drizzle of brown butter. But feel free to harness your inner Gianni and garnish more lavishly.

This polenta is enriched by the Parmesan broth and will hold nicely, over low heat, for a long time—if you're serving it as a side dish to a main that's still cooking away.

1 cup plus 1 tablespoon rustic polenta integrale or coarse-grind polenta (see page 72)

5 cups Parmesan Brodo (page 76; see Note)

1 tablespoon heavy cream

½ cup fresh ricotta

¼ cup finely grated Montasio cheese

⅛ cup crumbled Gorgonzola

¼ cup unsalted butter

In a sauté pan over high heat, toast the polenta until it turns a light golden color and takes on a very strong aroma of toasting corn, 2 to 3 minutes. Remove it from the heat and set aside. Reserve 1 tablespoon of the toasted polenta for the garnish.

In a heavy pot or Dutch oven over medium-high heat, bring the brodo to a boil. Slowly pour in the 1 cup polenta, letting it run in thin streams through your fingers while whisking constantly to avoid any clumping. Continue to whisk until the starch in the corn begins to release and the polenta starts to thicken. Bring the mixture to a boil, still whisking nonstop. Once the polenta starts to bubble and thicken slightly, after about 5 minutes, turn the heat to low and cover. Simmer for 45 to 60 minutes, whisking vigorously every 10 minutes or so, making sure to scrape the bottom and sides of the pot. The polenta will still have a small bit of texture left to it; this is what we want.

Meanwhile, bring a medium saucepan of water to a simmer.

In a heatproof bowl, combine the cream, ricotta, Montasio, and Gorgonzola. Place over but not touching the simmering water and stir well until melted and creamy. Keep this crema warm.

In a small saucepan over medium heat, melt the butter and cook until brown and nutty-smelling, about 3 minutes.

Transfer the cooked polenta to a shallow platter. Spoon the crema over the polenta, followed by a drizzle of the brown butter and a sprinkling of the reserved toasted polenta. Serve immediately.

Parmesan Brodo

Makes about 2½ quarts

Most people discard Parmesan rinds after all the cheese has been grated away, forgetting that there is still great flavor to be had. This is a deceptively simple broth that packs a punch. It is difficult to make this recipe in small quantities, as you need a decent amount of Parmesan scraps to develop good flavor. Don't be afraid to ask your cheesemonger or Italian deli counter (or both!) to save you some rinds. This recipe produces twice the amount you will need for Toc' in Braide, but it keeps well.

3 pounds Parmesan rinds or scraps

3½ quarts water

In a heavy pot or Dutch oven over medium-high heat, combine the Parmesan rinds and water. Bring to a boil, then lower the heat and simmer very gently, uncovered, for 5 hours, stirring every once in a while to dislodge any melted rinds from the bottom of the pot. Strain the broth, discarding the rinds. Store in an airtight container, in the refrigerator, for up to 5 days, or in the freezer, for up to 3 months.

ROSA DI GORIZIA, APPLE, AND HORSERADISH SALAD

Makes 4 to 6 servings

The climate and the alluvial soil around Gorizia is famous for being conducive to growing a red radicchio that has long been cultivated in the town's market gardens and surrounding agricultural fields (particularly Sant'Andrea and San Rocco). The radicchio looks like a rosebud about to open and is known as the *rosa di Gorizia*, "Gorizia rose." Indeed, bunched together, it's tough to tell this delicate lettuce from a bouquet from your local florist—the leaves are an intense, bright pink color, almost magenta, with shadings of garnet and white. The area's farmers have always grown this type of radicchio, and the region's menus buzz with the first harvest, like they do during the short asparagus season. We visited growers in late January, just after harvest, but there were still pink lettuces blossoming from the earth. For this radicchio, seedlings are planted in late summer, maturation begins in November and December, and harvest is in January and February.

To enjoy this recipe, January and February are your best bets, freshness-wise.

Note

Rosa di Gorizia can be found at the Union Square Greenmarket in New York City; look for the Campo Rosso Farm stand and its great chicories and radicchios. Or contact specialty Italian foods importer Alma Gourmet. Rosa del Veneto, another kind of radicchio, can also be found at specialty greengrocers and is a wonderful alternative.

YOU WILL NEED
Microplane zester/grater

2 Honeycrisp apples, peeled

1½ cups grated Montasio cheese

8 heads Rosa di Gorizia radicchio

½ cup olive oil

2 to 3 teaspoons red wine vinegar

1 tablespoon freshly grated horseradish, plus more for garnish

¾ teaspoon fine sea salt

With a box grater, using the side with the large holes, grate the apples into a medium bowl. Place the grated apples in the center of each plate so they are spread out a few inches wide. On top of the apples, sprinkle the grated Montasio, dividing it evenly among the plates.

Using a vegetable peeler, peel the outer stem of the radicchio to remove any tough brown exterior. Then, with a paring knife, cut the stem in half and split the remaining leafy parts by hand. If the heads are larger than 4 inches, cut into quarters.

In a large sauté pan over medium-low heat, combine the olive oil and all the radicchio. Rotate the radicchio a few times until the leaves soften, 3 to 4 minutes. Drizzle in the vinegar, sprinkle with the horseradish, and season with the salt.

Spoon the radicchio over the grated cheese and apple and Microplane some fresh horseradish on top of each plate. Serve immediately.

Rosa di Gorizia with a Warm Guanciale Vinaigrette

When you want something more exotic than the straight-forward Rosa di Gorizia, Apple, and Horseradish Salad, prepare Rosa di Gorizia with a warm guanciale vinaigrette.

In a large sauté pan over medium heat, combine ½ cup olive oil and 1 cup thinly sliced guanciale that has been cut coarsely into ½-inch squares. Cook until the guanciale is golden brown, 3 to 5 minutes.

While the guanciale is cooking, cut the roots from 8 heads of Rosa di Gorizia radicchio and then peel off each leaf. Clean the leaves with water, pat dry, and arrange in four salad bowls.

When the guanciale is golden brown, spoon the warm fat and the guanciale over the salads. Each salad should have 12 to 15 pieces of guanciale and 2 tablespoons of oil from the pan. Drizzle the salads with ⅓ cup of red wine vinegar, then sprinkle with salt. Serve without tossing, and allow each person to mix on their own. The salad will stay warm that way and not wilt.

BURRATA WITH PEACH, TOMATO, WATERMELON, AND SUMMER HERBS

Makes 4 servings

While this dish is not technically a Friulian dish, it is 100 percent Frasca. In Boulder, the summer growing season is short but intense. We have become known for our dishes using the incredible peaches that ripen on the western slopes of Colorado. Nothing says *summer* like these peaches, and visitors often plan their trips to Colorado around Palisade peach season and the August festival that comes with it.

In a medium bowl, whisk together the vinegar and olive oil and then season with the fine sea salt and pepper. Set this dressing aside.

Place the burrata in center of a serving platter. Arrange the peaches, tomatoes, and watermelon around the fresh cheese. Drizzle the dressing over top and garnish with the basil and mint leaves, then season with a generous amount of Maldon sea salt and pepper. Serve immediately.

3 tablespoons red wine vinegar

¼ cup extra-virgin olive oil

½ teaspoon fine sea salt

Freshly ground black pepper

2 balls burrata, quartered

2 ripe peaches, pits removed and flesh cut into wedges

2 heirloom tomatoes, cored and cut into wedges

2 cups cubed seedless watermelon

¼ cup torn fresh basil leaves

¼ cup torn fresh mint leaves

Maldon sea salt

White asparagus from near Cormons, Collio

WHITE ASPARAGUS WITH MONTASIO AND SPINACH SAUCE

Makes 2 servings

White asparagus is a chlorophyll-deprived delicacy that you see on menus from the Netherlands and Belgium to France and Italy. Akin to truffle season in Piedmont, white asparagus season is just as important to Friuli. Restaurants gear up for the spring allotment, and chefs begin to dream up new ways to prepare this illustrious vegetable. Indeed, locals and tourists alike practically line up at places such as Al Grop in Tavagnacco (just outside of Udine) to savor the tender, elegant stalks alongside a glass of herbaceous Sauvignon Blanc. It's part of the rite of spring. We've spent the winter enjoying hearty dishes, drinking full-bodied whites and earthy reds; now, it's as if our bodies are biologically primed for the season, ready to down a glass of zippy Sauvignon Blanc and enjoy the tender delicacy of this dish.

8 spears white asparagus, peeled and trimmed

1 pound fresh spinach leaves

1 tablespoon cold unsalted butter, cubed small

3 tablespoons extra-virgin olive oil

Fine sea salt and freshly ground black pepper

2 tablespoons finely grated Montasio cheese

10 fresh chive flowers

Bring a large pot of salted water to a boil. Fill a large bowl with ice cubes and cold water to form an ice bath. Line a plate with paper towels.

When the water boils, add the asparagus and blanch for 30 seconds, then remove the stalks from the pot and transfer to the ice bath. Transfer the asparagus to the prepared plate, reserving the ice bath for the spinach.

Return the pot of salted water to a boil, then plunge the spinach into the water and stir, cooking for 1 minute. Use a wire-mesh strainer to transfer to the ice bath. Squeeze the spinach to remove any excess water.

Transfer the spinach to a high-speed blender, add the butter, and blend on high speed while slowly streaming in 1 tablespoon of the olive oil to emulsify the sauce. It may be necessary to add a little water to achieve a smooth and pourable sauce consistency. Pass through a fine-mesh sieve, season with salt and pepper, and transfer to a small saucepan and warm over medium-low heat.

Allow the blanched asparagus to come to room temperature prior to plating. Drizzle the remaining 2 tablespoons olive oil over the spears, season with salt and pepper, and then arrange four spears on each plate. Spoon the warm spinach sauce over the asparagus. Finish each plate with the Montasio and garnish with the chive flowers. Serve immediately.

SOFT CREAMY POLENTA

Makes 4 servings

This is a great base dish for everything from a simple *ragù bianco* (white sauce) in winter to some grilled zucchini in summer.

Note
Warm, cooked polenta will hold nicely, over low heat, for a long time—if you're serving it as a side dish and still working on the main course. Remember to stir it now and then.

1 cup rustic polenta integrale or coarse-grind polenta (see page 72)

5 cups water

½ teaspoon fine sea salt

1 tablespoon unsalted butter

2 tablespoons freshly grated Parmigiano-Reggiano cheese

In a sauté pan over high heat, toast the polenta until it turns a light golden color and takes on a very strong aroma of toasting corn, 2 to 3 minutes. (This step is optional but does enhance the aroma of the finished dish.) Remove from the heat and set aside.

In a heavy pot or Dutch oven over high heat, bring the water to a boil. Slowly pour in the polenta, letting it run in thin streams through your fingers while whisking constantly to avoid any clumping. Bring the mixture to a boil, still whisking nonstop. Once the polenta starts to bubble and thicken slightly, after about 5 minutes, turn the heat to low and cover. Simmer for 1 hour (or up to 2 hours—add a splash more water as needed—which will result in an even lovelier texture), whisking vigorously every 10 minutes or so, making sure to scrape the bottom and sides of the pot. The polenta will still have a small bit of texture left to it; this is what we want.

Stir in the salt, butter, and cheese. Serve immediately!

How to Make Pasta Dough from Scratch

This is the basic method for making pasta dough. When called for in a particular recipe, combine the ingredients and then roll out the dough with either a pasta machine or the pasta rolling attachment on your stand mixer.

Note: Milled in Italy, 00 flour is a wheat flour. The flour is graded using a "zero" rating—0 is coarse in texture (like semolina flour); 00 tends to be the run-of-the-mill flour, used in many applications; and 000 is almost as fine as cornstarch. Look for 00 flour in specialty groceries and Italy-centric establishments. We love 00 flour due to its fineness, but you can make pasta using all-purpose flour.

1. In the bowl of a food processor or stand mixer fitted with the dough hook attachment, combine the flour(s), egg yolks, olive oil, and water and pulse (or mix on low speed) until a rough dough starts to form, five to seven pulses, or 30 seconds with the machine running. Alternatively, combine the ingredients in a large bowl and mix with a fork. Transfer the dough to the kitchen counter or a clean surface and knead for 2 to 3 minutes, until the dough becomes smooth. Wrap the ball of dough in plastic wrap and let sit at room temperature for 45 to 60 minutes, or refrigerate overnight.

2. Heavily dust a baking sheet or your counter with semolina flour. Cut the dough into ½-inch-thick slices. Keep the dough covered. Working with one slice at a time, flatten it a little with the palm of your hand. Roll the dough through the widest roller setting of your pasta machine (or attachment, if you're using a stand mixer), dusting with flour along the way to ensure the dough doesn't stick; don't use too much flour or the dough will become dry. Fold the sheet of dough in half onto itself and roll it through this initial setting five to ten times, folding it again after each pass.

3. Change the machine setting to the next, more-narrow setting and roll the sheet through once. Continue to change the machine setting to the next, more-narrow setting and roll the sheet through. You'll notice your sheet will become longer and longer as you work it through each successive setting. Keep rolling until Setting 7 (or the second-to-last setting on most pasta machines) and the pasta is very thin. Set the pasta aside on the prepared baking sheet or counter, and cover with a damp, clean tea towel. Repeat the rolling procedure with the remaining slices of dough.

4. When all of the pasta has been rolled into sheets, follow the recipe method for cutting instructions.

WHITE TRUFFLE TAJARIN

Makes 4 to 6 servings

Tajarin ("tie-yah-REEN") are the typical thin egg-yolk noodles of Piedmont; a high ratio of egg yolk gives the pasta its rich vibrant hue and renders the noodle extra-tender. Traditionally, the recipe calls for 40 egg yolks per 1 kilogram (2.2 pounds) of flour, but we have simplified this version. *Tajarin* is also Piedmontese for "tagliolini," but you see tajarin all across northern Italy. There is an Italian saying that states "No tajarin can ever be too rich or too thin!" We like ours about ⅛ inch wide.

And while people mostly associate white truffles with Alba, white truffles and truffles in general, stretch across many parts of Italy; you can find them in Tuscany and Friuli, as well as Slovenia, and even in Croatia. While Friuli is not internationally recognized for its white truffles, they're still a delicacy that's enjoyed there during the winter months.

Notes

Fresh white truffles are in season from November to January. If you don't have a specialty greengrocer near you, order them from www.dartagnan.com.

If using a tagliatelle cutter, pass the sheets of pasta through it. Dust the pasta with the semolina flour and twist it into a nest before setting on a baking sheet or a rack to dry.

YOU WILL NEED

Pasta machine or stand mixer fitted with pasta attachment
Mandoline

2 cups 00 flour (see Note, facing page)

10 egg yolks

1 tablespoon extra-virgin olive oil

¼ cup water, plus more as needed

Semolina flour for dusting

¾ cup unsalted butter

1 ounce white Alba truffle, cleaned with a brush

1 cup freshly grated Parmigiano-Reggiano cheese

Combine the 00 flour, egg yolks, olive oil, and water to make a dough as instructed on the facing page, dusting with semolina flour while rolling it into sheets of pasta.

Using a sharp knife, cut the rolled-out pasta sheets into 9-inch lengths.

Spread out the sheets of rolled dough on the flour-dusted counter, dusting them lightly with flour. Overlap two sheets of pasta and roll them into a cigar shape. Use the knife to slice the cigar into ⅛-inch-wide pieces. Using your hands, loosen the strands of pasta, dust with semolina flour, twist into a nest shape, and transfer to a floured baking sheet or a rack.

Bring 6 quarts of heavily salted water to a boil. Dust off any excess flour and drop the pasta into the boiling water. Give a gentle stir and cook for about 2 minutes after the water has returned to a vigorous simmer and the pasta is al dente. Drain completely.

While the pasta cooks, in a large sauté pan over medium-low heat, melt the butter. Toss the drained noodles in the melted butter and remove from the heat. Using a mandoline, shave half of the truffle into the noodles, add the Parmigiano, and toss gently to combine.

Divide the pasta among warm bowls and top each portion with more shavings of fresh truffle. Serve immediately.

ŽLIKROFI WITH VEAL JUS

Makes 4 to 6 servings; about 40 dumplings

Žlikrofi ("ZHLEE-krow-fee") are traditional Slovenian dumplings with a potato filling that originate from the town of Idrija. This is one of the dishes we often see served in the Collio, right on the border of Slovenia. It highlights the fact that Friuli is the western part of the Slavic world, and the southern part of the Austrian region. The dish was awarded protected geographic status by the European Union; it's that important to the culture.

If you are willing to make both this dish and Stinko di Vitello (page 121), together they create a meal that will pay off in spades. Spoon the pan juices and all the vegetables from the veal *over* this dish as the sauce. The flavor is incredibly rich.

Notes

Look for reduced veal stock at your local butcher shop.

Recipes often call for potatoes to be peeled by hand while still warm before passing them through a ricer. But in fact, warm boiled potatoes can be riced skin-on—the potato flesh passes through easily and the skin stays behind and can be easily lifted off and discarded.

YOU WILL NEED

Potato ricer
Pasta machine or stand mixer with pasta attachment
Pastry brush
Pizza wheel (optional)

ŽLIKROFI DOUGH

2 cups 00 flour
(see Note, page 88)

3 eggs

1 tablespoon extra-virgin
olive oil

POTATO FILLING

2 large Yukon gold potatoes

2 tablespoons olive oil

1 shallot, minced

3 garlic cloves, minced

¼ pound pancetta,
finely chopped

Finely grated zest of 1 lemon

Kosher salt and freshly ground
black pepper

Semolina flower for dusting

VEAL JUS

1½ cups reduced veal stock

4 tablespoons cold
unsalted butter

Fine sea salt and freshly ground
black pepper

Extra-virgin olive oil for drizzling

continued

To make the dough: Combine the 00 flour, eggs, and olive oil according to the instructions on page 88, step 1.

To make the filling: Bring a large saucepan of salted water to a boil. Add the potatoes and cook until tender, about 30 minutes.

While the potatoes are cooking, in a frying pan over medium-low heat, warm the olive oil. Add the shallot and garlic and sauté gently until softened, 2 to 3 minutes. Stir in the pancetta and continue to cook until the pancetta becomes crispy, about 3 minutes more. Remove from the heat.

When the potatoes are tender, remove them from the pot and let cool slightly. Cut in half or quarters and rice the potatoes into a bowl, discarding the skin leftovers as you go.

Using a spatula, stir the shallot-pancetta mixture into the potato, followed by the lemon zest. Season with salt and pepper. (The filling can be made 1 day ahead and refrigerated.)

Scoop up 2 teaspoons of the filling at a time and, using your hands, gently roll into a ball. Set aside on a baking sheet. Continue with the rest of the filling. You should have about 40 balls.

Dust two baking sheets or the counter with semolina flour. Fill a small glass with water.

Slice the žlikrofi dough into fourths. Roll out each piece of dough as detailed on page 88, steps 2 to 3, to its thinnest setting or just under—you should be able to see the dusting of flour through your pasta sheet when it lies on the counter. Set aside on a prepared baking sheet or the counter and keep covered. You should have four pasta sheets, 30 inches long by 5 inches wide.

Working on a lightly floured counter, lay out one sheet of pasta. Place balls of filling in a straight line onto the dough, 2 inches apart and about 1½ inches from the bottom edge (how many balls you can fit will depend on how long your sheet is, but eight or nine balls). Brush the space between each ball and the lengthwise edge above the balls with a little water. Pick up the bottom edge of the sheet of dough and carefully fold it snugly over all of the balls of filling, then use your hands to gingerly roll the plumped line of pasta over itself. Using a pizza wheel or a sharp knife, cut away any excess dough (lengthwise) beyond the seam. Cut the log at the halfway point between each mound of filling, then use the side edge of your hand to press down on either side of the mounds to mold the pasta snugly around each ball of filling and express any air trapped inside. Pick up one dumpling at a time and rotate it vertically away from you, using your thumb to press down firmly on the filling at the top fold/crease line—this will result in the žlikrofi's characteristic wrapped-candy shape, called *caramele*. Transfer to the second prepared baking sheet. Repeat with the remaining sheets of pasta dough and balls of filling. (The žlikrofi can be wrapped in plastic and refrigerated for up to 24 hours.)

Bring a large pot of salted water to a rolling boil.

To make the jus: In a medium saucepan over medium-high heat, bring the veal stock to a boil. Turn the heat to medium-low and simmer to reduce until the jus coats the back of a spoon (you can trace a line on the back of the spoon with your finger and it remains visible). The timing will depend on the viscosity/consistency of the jus you are using. Whisk in the butter, 1 tablespoon at a time, to form a glossy sauce. Season with salt and pepper and keep warm.

Add the dumplings to the boiling water and cook for 3 minutes after the water returns to a consistent simmer and then, using a slotted spoon or skimmer, gently transfer to a large bowl, or place five or six žlikrofi in individual bowls. Drizzle veal jus over each portion, followed by a drizzle of extra-virgin olive oil. Serve immediately.

Near Brazzano, Gorizia

La Subida

La Subida in Cormons in the Collio is our Friulian home away from home. It is the idyllic countryside inn of our dreams. In 1947, owner Pepe Sirk moved from Slovenia to Cormons, Italy—a whole eight kilometers away. He bought a field with a farmhouse that still stands today. Post-war Italy of the late 1940s and early '50s was a difficult place, and many farming communities were hit hard. Since farming was not enough to sustain Pepe and his family, they opened their home as what would be one of the first frascas in the area.

In 1952, Jŏsko Sirk was born—a surprise for his mother at the age of fifty. She gave him a Slovenian name since they were a Slovenian family. When Pepe went to register the name at the local town hall, he was denied; at that time, all children born within Italian borders were mandated to have an Italian name. "To you he can be Jŏsko, but his name is officially Andreano," they were told.

Jŏsko took over the family farm at the age of twenty. In 1977, he married Loredana, a beautiful woman from the Carso who was studying medicine. And this is when the dream of having a restaurant began. The idea was to create an intense sense of hospitality—not to simply serve people. They wanted to cook in a more innovative way, but still according to Friulian tradition. During this time, there were vineyards on the (always expanding) property, and so Jŏsko, being the evergreen innovator, began making wine. In 1980, his first daughter, Tanja, was born. Two more children followed quickly on her heels: Erika and then a son, Mitja.

For the first twenty years, the family's apartment was located above the restaurant. La Subida was always meant to have a connection with family and nature, a philosophy that is deeply embedded in Jŏsko. In the late '90s, the family decided to innovate even more and created a new menu designed to connect their culture, emotions, and the terroir to the food in a progressive and healthful way. Jŏsko hired Friulian chef Alessandro "Sandro" Gavagna to cook what was essentially fresh-market Friulian food. It worked out well, as Sandro is now officially part of the Sirk family, having married Tanja.

La Subida has always been a sort of winemaker's canteen. It is often the reason people visit. When Jŏsko began building his restaurant cellar, he wanted to provide the best of the region, give some options from outside of Friuli and Italy, and have a collection that runs deep with age.

He has far exceeded his goals, in our opinion. And his son, Mitja, who now makes his own wine, is fast becoming one of Italy's best wine minds. (That's how growing up at La Subida affects you.) Mitja is in charge of the cellar now, along with his fiancée, Marta Venica, a great wine intellect in her own right. There is always a new project happening at La Subida. It is the Sirk family's life's work, and when you visit, you feel like part of the bigger family too.

BUCKWHEAT BLECS WITH CHICKEN AND ROSEMARY

Makes 6 to 8 servings

Friuli offers some extreme varieties of pasta (indeed, we considered calling this book *Weird Pasta Shapes!*), which brings us to *blecs*. Made with a sifted mix of buckwheat and wheat flours, this pasta is typically cut into triangles or squares.

This dish is so much more than the sum of its parts—the chicken has surprising depth of flavor thanks to being braised alongside rosemary and an onion. That flavor is supported by the dark and earthy buckwheat pasta triangles. It's full-on rustic with restaurant-grade flavor. There is no nice way to say it: This dish is ugly. But we promise making and eating it will convince any naysayers.

Notes

Because the braising liquid is reduced to make a final sauce, the chicken stock should be homemade or butcher-bought and salt-free. Do not be tempted to use supermarket stock or low-sodium broth—the resulting dish will be too salty.

You can make the pasta ahead of time, transfer it to a well-floured tray, wrap tightly in plastic, and refrigerate overnight.

YOU WILL NEED

Pasta machine or stand mixer fitted with pasta attachment
Fluted pastry wheel

PASTA DOUGH

1 cup 00 flour (see Note, page 88)	2 eggs, plus 1 egg yolk
⅓ cup buckwheat flour	1 teaspoon extra-virgin olive oil
	Semolina flour for dusting

BRAISED CHICKEN

Fine sea salt and freshly ground black pepper	1 medium yellow onion, cut into ⅛-inch-thick rounds
1 whole chicken, cut into 8 pieces	½ cup dry white wine
¼ cup olive oil	2 cups unsalted chicken stock
	2 rosemary sprigs

Extra-virgin olive oil for drizzling

continued

To make the dough: Combine the 00 flour, buckwheat flour, eggs and egg yolk, and olive oil, according to the instructions on page 88, step 1.

Dust a baking sheet with semolina flour. Roll out the pasta dough according to the instructions on page 88, but stopping at setting 5 rather than 7, or a thickness of $\frac{1}{16}$ inch—the blecs tend to be a little more rustic than, say, delicate ravioli. Lay the pasta on the prepared baking sheet. Repeat the rolling procedure with the remaining slices of dough.

Dust a work surface with semolina flour and spread out the sheets of rolled dough. Using a fluted pastry wheel, cut the pasta sheets into long 2-inch-wide strips, then cut each strip into triangles with two equal sides (isosceles triangles). Transfer the triangles to the prepared baking sheet and set aside.

To make the chicken: Generously salt and pepper the chicken pieces.

In a large Dutch oven over medium-high heat, warm the olive oil. Add the chicken and sear on both sides until golden brown, about 5 minutes, working in batches as necessary. Remove the chicken from the pot and set aside.

Add the onion to the same pot and brown until caramelized, about 15 minutes—resisting the urge to stir too much. Turn the heat to high, pour in the white wine, stirring well to incorporate all the brown bits at the bottom of the pot, and reduce by half, about 2 minutes.

Return the chicken pieces to the pot, pour in the chicken stock, and add the rosemary sprigs. Bring to a simmer, then cover and braise for 25 to 30 minutes, until the chicken is cooked through. Transfer the chicken from the pot to a plate. Reduce the chicken stock until slightly thickened, about 10 minutes.

Meanwhile, fill a pot with heavily salted water and bring to a boil.

Separate the chicken meat from the bones and return the shredded meat and the skin to the sauce. Cover and keep warm.

Add the pasta to the boiling water and cook until tender, about 3 minutes after the water has returned to a vigorous simmer. Strain in a colander, reserving $\frac{1}{2}$ cup (or more) of the cooking liquid in case the chicken sauce needs loosening.

Stir the cooked blecs into the chicken sauce, mixing well, adding starchy cooking water as needed, if you find the sauce too thick. Transfer to individual plates and drizzle with extra-virgin olive oil. Serve immediately.

WOVEN LASAGNA WITH SPINACH SAUCE

Makes 6 servings

There is perhaps no other pasta dish that has caught my attention as much as this one. It combines flavor, finesse, and a very creative presentation. The first time we came across this woven-then-sliced lasagna was at a lunch with the entire Frasca team—on one of our staff journeys to Friuli in 2007—at La Primula in the small village of San Quirino (northwest of Trieste). In true Friuli style, the restaurant's lasagna included prosciutto di San Daniele! We have since made this type of lasagna with meat ragù or mushroom ragù. All of these options make for playful and delicious alternatives. The recipe here, though, is the original one we all enjoyed at La Primula.

Note

The lasagna is best assembled the day before serving and refrigerated overnight, before slicing and heating. The spinach sauce can also be made ahead and reheated. So, this impressive and visually elegant dish comes together in mere minutes the day-of!

YOU WILL NEED
Pasta machine or stand mixer fitted with pasta attachment
9 by 5-inch loaf pan
Piping bag fitted with large plain tip

LASAGNA DOUGH

2 ½ cups 00 flour (see Note, page 88)	1 tablespoon extra-virgin olive oil
2 eggs, plus 3 egg yolks	

Extra-virgin olive oil for drizzling

PROSCIUTTO-RICOTTA FILLING

One ¼-inch slice prosciutto di San Daniele, finely cubed	¾ cup freshly grated Parmigiano-Reggiano cheese
1 tablespoon extra-virgin olive oil	2 teaspoons minced fresh rosemary
2½ cups whole-milk ricotta	Fine sea salt

SPINACH SAUCE

10 ounces baby spinach	Extra-virgin olive oil for drizzling
Fine sea salt	

½ cup freshly grated Parmigiano-Reggiano cheese

To make the dough: Combine the 00 flour, eggs and egg yolks, and olive oil, according to the instructions on page 88, and roll it into two pasta sheets only. The sheets should be approximately 32 inches long by 5 inches wide (you will have some leftover dough, which you can cut, cook, and enjoy with your favorite pasta sauce).

Bring a large pot of salted water to a boil. Generously drizzle a baking sheet with olive oil to prevent sticking.

continued

Add a pasta sheet to the boiling water and cook for 1 minute after the water has returned to a simmer. Using a spider and any other large spoon or spatula, gently scoop up the pasta, transfer it to the prepared baking sheet and arrange flat, with some overlapping, using your hands. Drizzle some more olive oil over the top. Cook the second sheet of pasta in the simmering water and repeat the process. Set aside.

To make the filling: In a food processor, pulse the prosciutto cubes until they take on the texture of ground meat.

In a medium frying pan over medium heat, warm the olive oil. Add the prosciutto and cook, stirring occasionally until crispy, about 5 minutes. Transfer to paper towels to drain and let cool.

In a medium bowl, combine the ricotta, Parmigiano, rosemary, and prosciutto. Season with salt and transfer to a piping bag fitted with a large plain tip.

Oil a loaf pan.

Lay the first sheet of pasta lengthways across the width of the prepared loaf pan—one end of the pasta should be overlapping the long edge of the pan by 5 inches, the (very long) rest of the sheet should be hanging over the other edge. Press on the pasta to line the bottom of the pan. Repeat with the second sheet on the other end of the pan, overlapping it slightly with the first sheet as needed. Pipe a line of filling along the long edge of the pan, right up against the edge. Leave a 1-inch space before piping a second parallel line of filling down the length of the pan. There should be a 1-inch space on either side of this line of filling. Carefully fold the long end of each pasta sheet over the filling, pressing down with your fingers to make the pasta hug both lines of filling and let the extra pasta drape over the other edge of the pan. Repeat the piping in the two hollow trenches you've just formed by pressing down on the pasta with your hands. Drape the sheets of pasta back over the filling to the other side, pressing down to smooth.

Next, once again pipe a line of filling along the long edge of the pan, right up against the edge. Leave a 1-inch space before piping a second parallel line of filling down the length of the pan. As before, there should be a 1-inch space on either side of this line of filling. Carefully fold the long end of each pasta sheet over the filling, pressing down with your fingers to make the pasta hug both lines of filling and let the extra pasta drape over the other edge of the pan. Repeat the piping in the two hollow trenches you've just formed with your hands. Drape the sheets of pasta back over the filling to the other side, pressing down to smooth. Use a sharp knife or scissors to trim the excess pasta—then fold the short edge of the pasta sheet down over it. Wrap in plastic and refrigerate for at least 6 hours or up to overnight.

Preheat the oven to 450°F. Line a baking sheet with parchment paper.

To make the sauce: Bring 5 cups of salted water to a boil. Fill a large bowl with ice cubes and cold water to form an ice bath.

Add the spinach to the boiling water and cook until wilted but still green, about 2 minutes. Transfer to the ice bath to cool. Drain gently, skimming the ice off the top. Resist the urge to squeeze out all the excess liquid from the spinach. Using tongs, transfer the spinach to a high-speed blender and puree, adding up to ¼ cup water as needed to loosen the sauce to a pouring consistency—you should have about 1½ cups. Season with salt and a drizzle of extra-virgin olive oil. Keep warm.

Unmold the lasagna onto a cutting board and cut into six 1½-inch-wide slices. Lay the slices flat on the prepared baking sheet and sprinkle each with about 1 tablespoon grated Parmigiano. Bake until golden-brown and slightly puffed, with some browning along the edges of the pasta, 10 to 12 minutes.

Spoon just over 3 tablespoons of spinach sauce onto the center of each plate and spread out in a circle using the back of the spoon. Lay a slice of the lasagna on top of each circle. Serve immediately.

TAGLIOLINI AL PORTONAT

(Tagliolini in a Prosciutto and Poppy Seed Cream Sauce)

Makes 6 servings

There is no better incarnation of this pasta dish than the one we enjoyed at Osteria Al Portonat in San Daniele, the famed hilltop village—until now. Possibly one of the easiest *primi* (first courses) to make, this pasta is completely unique, in large part due to the addition of poppy seeds, which give the dish a kind of Friulian carbonara feel.

Like most Italian food, this tagliolini consists of just a few ingredients of the highest quality, prepared simply and with respect for the age-old cooking techniques of the region. If you can find a nice piece of prosciutto di San Daniele, this pasta will make you feel like you're eating lunch in the lower foothills of the Carnic Alps. It's guaranteed to become a standard in your pasta repertoire. The trick here is to render the prosciutto quickly but gently; cooking it for too long or too hard ruins the melt-in-your-mouth texture.

Notes

Prosciutto di San Daniele DOP makes this dish soar. Do not be tempted to substitute a different prosciutto. Find it at Eataly, Whole Foods, and most reputable delis or cheese shops.

If dried tagliolini (a narrower version of tagliatelle) proves hard to find, substitute De Cecco's squared spaghetti or Rustichella d'Abruzzo's chitarra.

Two ¼-inch-thick slices prosciutto di San Daniele, plus 6 thin slices

1 pound dry tagliolini pasta

¼ cup extra-virgin olive oil

1 cup heavy cream

1 tablespoon poppy seeds, plus more for sprinkling

Fine sea salt

Freshly ground black pepper

Cut the thick prosciutto slices into ¼-inch cubes. Set aside.

Bring a large pot of salted water to a boil. Add the pasta and cook until al dente (see package for timing instructions).

While the pasta is cooking, in a sauté pan over medium-low heat, warm the olive oil. Add the cubed prosciutto and sauté it until lightly browned, about 3 minutes. Add the cream and simmer until reduced to a thick sauce, 7 to 10 minutes.

Drain the pasta and then toss in the pan with the cream and prosciutto. Add the poppy seeds and toss again. Check the seasoning, adding salt, if needed.

Transfer the pasta to one platter, family-style (or divide among six plates), sprinkling with a grind or two of black pepper and a few poppy seeds. Drape the thin prosciutto slices over the top of the pasta. Serve immediately.

TAGLIATELLE AL RAGÙ BIANCO

(Tagliatelle in a White Ragu)

Makes 4 to 6 servings

This dish has an amazing depth of flavor that comes from four very simple ingredients: chicken stock, fresh rosemary, onion, and beef. The pasta is a beautiful golden color, thanks to all the egg yolks in the dough. Ragùs without tomatoes are often served in the north of Italy, and represent Friuli at its best. Kelly Jeun and Eduardo Valle Lobo, the executive chefs at Frasca, lived in Friuli for a couple of years; cooking this dish sends them right back to the warm memories they have from their time there.

Note

Because the chicken stock used to braise the beef is reduced to make a final sauce, it should be homemade or butcher-bought and salt-free. Do not be tempted to use supermarket stock or low-sodium broth—the resulting dish will be too salty.

YOU WILL NEED

Pasta machine or stand mixer fitted with pasta attachment

TAGLIATELLE DOUGH

1½ cups 00 flour (see Note, page 88)	10 egg yolks
½ cup semolina flour, plus more for dusting	1 tablespoon extra-virgin olive oil
	¼ cup water

RAGÙ BIANCO

¼ cup olive oil	1 teaspoon fine sea salt
1 large onion, finely diced	2 rosemary sprigs
1 pound ground beef	1 cup unsalted chicken stock
1 cup freshly grated Parmigiano-Reggiano cheese	Fine sea salt and freshly ground black pepper

To make the dough: Combine the 00 flour, semolina flour, egg yolks, olive oil, and water according to the instructions on page 88, step 1.

To make the ragù: While the pasta dough rests, in a large Dutch oven or heavy pot over medium-low heat, warm the olive oil. Add the onion and sweat, covered, until translucent, about 10 minutes, stirring occasionally.

Add the ground beef to the pot and stir to it break up, then cover and cook through, 7 to 10 minutes more. Add the salt, rosemary sprigs, and chicken stock and bring to a simmer, then cover and let stew for 10 to 15 minutes, allowing the flavors to mingle. Keep warm over very low heat.

Roll out the pasta dough into thin sheets according to the instructions on page 88, steps 2 to 5.

Spread the sheets of rolled dough on the flour-dusted counter and dust lightly with flour. Overlap two sheets of pasta and roll into a cigar shape. Use a sharp knife to slice the pasta into ⅓-inch-wide pieces. Using your hands, loosen the strands of pasta, dust with semolina flour, twist into a nest shape, and transfer to a floured baking sheet or rack.

Bring 6 quarts of heavily salted water to a boil.

Dust off any excess flour and drop the pasta into the boiling water. Give a gentle stir and cook for about 3 minutes after the water has returned to a vigorous simmer, or until the pasta is al dente. Strain the pasta, reserving 1 cup of the cooking liquid.

Add the noodles to the ragù, toss, and cook for 1 minute over medium-low heat. Remove from the heat, discard the rosemary sprig, and stir in the grated Parmigiano. Use some of the reserved cooking water as needed to loosen the sauce. Adjust the seasoning with salt and pepper.

Divide the pasta among warm bowls and serve immediately.

CHICKEN MARCUNDELA WITH CHERRY MOSTARDA AND POTATO PUREE

Makes 4 servings

Marcundela exemplifies the nose-to-tail ethos that Italian cooks have always favored; traditionally, this sausage is prepared with ground meat made from the pork bits and offal left over at the end of a pig slaughter and is wrapped in caul fat. At least, that's often how you see it served throughout FVG. However, one night during dinner at La Subida, we had a poultry version that was so good we decided to replicate it here, with a spicy cherry mostarda and potato puree. If you opt out of using the caul fat, you could instead sprinkle the cooked ground meat atop a salad or pasta, like the squash gnocchi on page 218.

YOU WILL NEED

Meat grinder fitted with medium die (¼ inch/6mm), stand mixer with meat grinder attachment, or food processor
Digital scale (optional)
Potato ricer (optional)
Instant-read digital thermometer

CHICKEN MARCUNDELA

1 pound boneless, skinless chicken thighs	⅛ teaspoon ground star anise
¼ pound chicken livers, soaked in milk for 30 minutes	⅛ teaspoon freshly grated nutmeg
¼ pound chicken hearts	2 tablespoons red wine
⅛ teaspoon ground cloves	1 teaspoon fine sea salt
⅛ teaspoon ground cinnamon	½ teaspoon freshly ground black pepper
⅛ teaspoon ground ginger	7 ounces caul fat, kept in cold water

CHERRY MOSTARDA

1 pound Bing cherries, pitted	3 tablespoons whole-grain Dijon mustard
½ cup sugar	
½ cup white balsamic vinegar	
¼ teaspoon fine sea salt	

POTATO PUREE

1 ½ pounds Yukon gold potatoes (see Note, page 91)	2 tablespoons unsalted butter, melted
	Fine sea salt
2 tablespoons extra-virgin olive oil	

To make the marcundela: Cut the chicken thighs, livers, and hearts into ½-inch cubes. Pass them through a meat grinder fitted with a medium die into a bowl. Alternatively, you can pulse the meat mixture nine or ten times in a food processor until amalgamated and coarsely ground, then transfer to a bowl. Stir in the cloves, cinnamon, ginger, star anise, nutmeg, red wine, salt, and pepper.

Squeeze the caul fat to remove excess water. Working on a cutting board, gently spread out the caul fat pieces (sizes and shapes will vary). Scoop ¼ cup of the meat mixture out of the bowl and onto the caul fat. Repeat with the rest of the meat mixture, ¼ cup at a time, leaving about 2 inches of caul fat around each patty. Don't worry too much if it looks like you don't have enough caul fat—it's very stretchy and forgiving.

Using a sharp knife, cut a square of caul fat around each patty. Lift and gently stretch the caul fat to wrap it around each patty, then transfer the patty, seam-side down, to a plate. Refrigerate for 1 hour, or up to 6 hours, before cooking.

To make the mostarda: In a heavy saucepan over medium-high heat, combine the cherries, sugar, vinegar, salt, and mustard. Bring to a boil, turn the heat to medium-low, and simmer vigorously, stirring regularly, until the cherries have softened and the juices are syrupy, 30 to 40 minutes. Set aside to cool.

To make the potato puree: Fill a large pot with 6 quarts of heavily salted cold water. Add the potatoes, bring to a boil, and then simmer until the potatoes are tender when poked with a paring knife, 35 to 40 minutes, depending on the size of your potatoes.

Once cooked, peel the potatoes while still warm and press them through a ricer for a smooth texture, or mash them with a potato masher for a chunkier texture. Whisk in the melted butter and season with salt. Keep warm.

In a large nonstick frying pan over medium-high heat, warm the olive oil. Gently place the marcundela seam-side down in the pan—work in two batches if your pan is not large enough. Turn the heat to medium after 2 minutes and continue to cook for 6 minutes, until browned on that side, then flip the marcundela and cook until a digital thermometer registers an internal temperature of 165°F, another 3 to 4 minutes.

Dollop a generous amount of potato puree onto each plate and top with one or two marcundela. Pour a spoonful or two of cherry mostarda over each sausage. Serve immediately.

PHEASANT WITH FENNEL AND APPLES

Makes 4 servings

Hunting pheasant, deer, and boar is a big part of the culture in Friuli. On top of Castel Monte, just north of Cividale, you'll find La Planina, a small restaurant with a chef who personally hunts the pheasant for the ragù he likes to serve with gnocchi. As he would rather be out in the woods, his restaurant is mostly open only on weekends. But the gnocchi are spectacular, served with either porcini or pheasant.

Pheasant can often be a little dry and is tricky to cook, so pay attention to get the doneness just right. We prepare the pheasant on the bone and braise it in stock to keep the meat moist.

Note
Order pheasant online from www.dartagnan.com, or buy it from a butcher who specializes in game meat.

¼ cup olive oil,
plus 3 tablespoons

One 2- to 2½-pound pheasant, halved

Fine sea salt and freshly ground black pepper

1 garlic head, halved

½ yellow onion, cut into ½-inch dice

½ celery rib, cut into ½-inch dice

½ carrot, peeled and cut into ½-inch dice

1 cup red wine

1 dried bay leaf

2 thyme sprigs

2 to 4 cups chicken stock or low-sodium chicken broth

2 medium fennel bulbs, halved lengthwise, cored, and cut into sixths

2 medium Granny Smith apples, peeled, cored, and cut into 6 wedges

In a large Dutch oven over medium heat, warm the ¼ cup olive oil. Season the pheasant halves with salt and pepper. Add one pheasant half to the pot and sear on both sides until nicely browned, 6 to 8 minutes. Set aside. Sear the second half, then set aside. Add the garlic, onion, celery, and carrot to the pot and brown the vegetables until caramelized, about 10 minutes. Add the red wine, deglaze the pot, scraping up any browned bits with a wooden spoon, and reduce until thick, about 5 minutes. Add the bay leaf and thyme.

Return the pheasant halves to the pot and cover with the chicken stock (the amount you use will depend on the size of your pot). Bring to a boil, then cover, turn the heat to low, and simmer gently until the pheasant is tender, about 40 minutes. Transfer the pheasant to a tray or large plate.

Bring the cooking broth back to a boil over high heat, then turn the heat to medium-low and simmer until slightly thickened, about 7 minutes. Season with salt and pepper. Return the pheasant to the pot, cover, and keep warm.

In large frying pan over medium heat, warm the remaining 3 tablespoons olive oil. Add the fennel wedges and cook for 5 minutes, stirring occasionally, then add the apple wedges and cook for another 5 minutes. Season with salt.

Cut each pheasant half into two pieces, arrange on a shallow serving platter, spoon the sauce over, and garnish with the fennel and apple pieces. Serve immediately.

The Answer Is the Flywheel (The Snaidero Slicer)

Mirco Snaidero's workshop sits on the edge of San Daniele in the suburb of Colloredo di Monte Albano. To enter it is to enter into his mind. There is not a speck of dust, nor a drop of oil; and not a single tool, of the thousands there, is out of place. Sure, there is an Ayrton Senna poster from his Lotus Formula One racing days, and the odd Pirelli calendar, but every other thing in the room has a purpose: precision. Minute detail reigns supreme here; it could be the workshop of an OCD mechanic. And it kind of is. This is where Snaidero prosciutto slicers, the Rolls-Royce of ham slicers, are hand-built and custom-made. If you take ham-slicing seriously, or even just love a beautifully built object, this is your Valhalla. It's ours too.

Snaidero is a family business that includes Mirco (pictured bottom right with Lachlan), his wife, Alida, their daughter, Karin, and son, Gary. In 2009, we were introduced to these extremely passionate and proud Friulians, and we placed our first order in 2010. Considering the amount of prosciutto we slice nightly at Frasca, it was a complete dream to have the Berkel Model 22 wide-carriage slicer in our restaurant dining room. If Frasca were a showroom, the Snaidero is our Maserati. Each slicer takes one month to build, and there is a six-month waiting list. We often see posts online from restaurateurs across America exclaiming about the delivery date for their new Snaidero slicer. *All this, over a ham slicer?!* Yep.

The story of Snaidero started in 1981, when Mirco was a mechanic. People brought him Motor Guzzi motorcycles to repair daily, but as the family lived a mere kilometer from San Daniele—home of the world's most famous prosciutto—people started bringing him slicers to fix.

Place plays *really* heavily here. If the Snaidero family had lived in Liguria, for example, this would not be the same story. After fixing a few slicers, Mirco began creating the parts himself, partly because the size made it complicated—many were Berkel models from England, which can be as big as a compact car—but mostly because the parts were difficult to obtain. His eureka moment happened in 1998. Mirco was still working on motorbikes when a friend offered to sell him 160 slicers. Mirco asked to think about it overnight. In the morning, he realized that he was satisfied with his level of success with motorbikes and was ready to take on something new. To be able to afford all the slicers, he sold his entire warehouse of motorbikes and Vespas.

Beyond the beauty and customization (hello, model S with notable green color and Friuli flag), there are two distinct elements that made a Snaidero special: a concave blade, designed so the prosciutto can be room temperature and never come into contact with the whole of the blade, and the flywheel, the operating wheel with a handle that denotes an artisan slicer. When Mirco decided to create his own slicer, he kept the simplicity of the Guzzi motorcycle—the only motorbike that has the flywheel on the exterior. Similar to a smoker, where the smoke finds its groove over time, the flywheel finds its slicing groove, especially with a bit of love from its operator. For us, simplicity, elegance, and the lightness of the mechanics define these slicers.

MUSETTO CON CIPOLLE ALL'ACETO

(Friulian Fresh Pork Sausage with Vinegar-Glazed Onions)

Makes 6 servings

Traditionally, *musetto* is freshly cooked pork sausage made from the head of the pig, similar to cottechino, but without the spices or the casing. It can be served with polenta or brovada, but it is most important to accompany it with a high-acid component, like a vinegar-based pan sauce or Cipolle all'Aceto, to cut through the richness of the meat. For this dish, we have adopted a technique that is normally used with fresh salami, which can be hard to find in the United States due to regulations about the levels of moisture deemed legal in raw meat.

We love this recipe so much that whenever we put on an event, we almost always cook musetto.

Hot Tip: If you're ever in Friuli, and you've had too many vineyard visits through the Collio, head to Udine to visit our friend Monica at Osteria Al Capello. She knows musetto over polenta is the best recipe to nurse you back to health (and get you ready for more tastings).

Notes

Making this sausage from scratch requires a great meat grinder and a good relationship with your butcher. Both pig skin and fatback may prove difficult to source; ask your butcher to remove and give you the skin from the pork belly you are buying and/or to keep any scraps for you. If your butcher doesn't have fatback in the freezer, make friends with your local charcuterie maker, who will most definitely have some.

If you don't want to grind the cooked skin, belly, and fatback at home, bring them back to your butcher (once you've cooked the skin) and ask him to pass the belly and fat through a meat grinder on the smaller setting, and the pork skin through a wider setting (a smaller setting may just turn the skin to mush).

YOU WILL NEED
Meat grinder fitted with medium die (¼ inch/6mm)
    or stand mixer with meat grinder attachment

½ pound pork skin	2 tablespoons unsalted butter
1 pound pork belly, skin removed, cold	6 thin slices prosciutto di San Daniele
¼ pound fatback, cold	¼ cup red wine vinegar
1 teaspoon fine sea salt	Soft Creamy Polenta (page 87) or Brovada (page 149) for serving
4 cups chicken stock or low-sodium chicken broth	
1 bay leaf	Cipolle all'Aceto (recipe follows) for serving

Bring a large pot of water to a boil. Add the pork skin and cook for 6 minutes. Transfer to a plate and refrigerate until cold.

Cut the pork belly and fatback into ½-inch cubes, then pass through a meat grinder. Cut the pork skin into ½-inch squares, then combine them with half of the ground belly and fat and grind that mixture together. Refrigerate the ground meat and fat for 30 minutes.

Combine the cold ground meat, skin, and fat and the salt in the bowl of a stand mixer fitted with the paddle attachment and mix on low speed for 2 minutes, until the mixture looks uniform and the fat has emulsified.

Divide the sausage meat into six portions (about 6 ounces each). Using your hands, shape into 6-inch logs, approximately 1 inch in diameter. Transfer to a plate. Wrap each log tightly in plastic, poking holes here and there with a cake tester or just the tip of a very sharp paring knife to release any air pockets. Refrigerate the meat until it firms up, about 30 minutes.

In a large saucepan over high heat, bring the chicken stock to a boil. Add the bay leaf and ease the wrapped musetto logs into the stock. Turn the heat to low and poach gently for 2 hours, until tender and fully cooked. Transfer the musetto to a plate and let rest for 5 to 7 minutes.

continued

Line a plate with paper towels.

While the musetto is resting, in a large frying pan over medium heat, melt the butter. Add the prosciutto slices, working in batches as needed, and cook until crispy, 2 to 3 minutes. Transfer the prosciutto to the prepared plate to drain. Turn the heat to low, add the vinegar, deglaze the pan, scraping up any browned bits with a wooden spoon, and set aside.

Move the sausages to a cutting board, unwrap, and slice into 1-inch coins. Transfer to a platter, along with polenta, the crispy prosciutto, and the cipolle all'aceto, drizzling the pan sauce over the meat. Serve immediately.

Cipolle all'Aceto
(Vinegar-Glazed Onions)

Makes 6 servings

These onions are a constant on menus throughout Friuli and, ergo, the mise-en-place at Frasca. Perfect for any meat or polenta that needs a hit of acid.

¼ cup olive oil	1 bay leaf
3 large yellow onions, cut into ½-inch-wide rings	⅓ cup high-quality white wine vinegar
Fine sea salt	

In a large Dutch oven over medium heat, warm the olive oil. Add the onions and sprinkle with 1 teaspoon salt. Add the bay leaf. Turn the heat to low, cover, and sweat the onions until translucent and soft, about 15 minutes, stirring once or twice. Add the vinegar and cook for 30 minutes, uncovered, stirring every 5 minutes or so, until the onions have fully caramelized. Remove the bay leaf and adjust the seasoning with salt. Store in an airtight container, in the refrigerator, for up to 3 days, and reheat slowly before serving.

Piazzo San Giacomo, Udine

ROAST PORK AND PEACHES

Makes 8 to 10 servings

Years ago, when Frasca Food and Wine first opened, we started the tradition of a Monday Night Wine Dinner; it was organized around a theme, most often a winemaker who worked with the kitchen to design a wine-pairing menu and then joined us to pour his or her bottles. One summer night at the height of peach season, we decided to serve a simple peach salad with roast pork featuring the wines of Livio Felluga. The wine flight consisted of a Friulano, Sauvignon Blanc, and Terre Alte. Little did we know that this dish would become a Frasca classic. Rather than focusing on technique, we were thinking about what people wanted to eat and drink on a warm August night. The lighter protein speaks of summer. We've since made this many ways, playing with how we cook the pork as well as the fruit pairings—cherries, pears, plums, and persimmons all work well, but peaches may be our favorite. This recipe feeds a crowd, and we suggest serving it family-style.

YOU WILL NEED
Mortar and pestle
Digital meat probe

4-pound boneless pork loin roast, tied

Fine sea salt and freshly ground black pepper

4 tablespoons olive oil

1 tablespoon minced fresh rosemary

1 tablespoon minced fresh thyme

6 garlic cloves, minced

10 fingerling potatoes

3 ripe peaches, peeled, quartered, and pitted

8 Cipollini onions, peeled and quartered

1 tablespoon Dijon mustard

Extra-virgin olive oil for drizzling

Preheat the oven to 350°F.

Pat the pork loin dry with paper towels. Season generously all over with salt and pepper.

In a mortar, use a pestle to combine 2 tablespoons of the olive oil, the rosemary, thyme, and garlic into a paste, then rub this mixture all over the meat.

In a large frying pan over medium-high heat, warm the remaining 2 tablespoons olive oil. Add the pork loin and sear, turning it several times, until nicely browned on all sides, 8 to 10 minutes total.

Insert a meat probe deep into the center of the meat, place the meat in a 9 by 13-inch baking dish, and transfer to the oven.

In a medium saucepan over high heat, cover the potatoes with water, add 1 tablespoon salt, and simmer until tender, about 25 minutes. Drain, use the back of a paring knife to peel off the skin, and then slice into ½-inch-thick coins.

Cut each peach wedge in half and set aside.

After the meat has been roasting for 45 minutes, add the onions and roast another 10 to 15 minutes, until the meat probe registers 140°F. Transfer the meat to a cutting board, tent with aluminum foil to keep warm, and let rest for 20 minutes.

Stir the mustard into the cooking juices and onions and season with salt and pepper. Add the potatoes and peaches and stir gently to coat with the warm dressing. Check the seasoning again, then generously drizzle extra-virgin olive oil over the top.

Cut the roast into ¼-inch-thick slices and transfer to a large platter; spoon the warm salad next to the meat. Serve immediately.

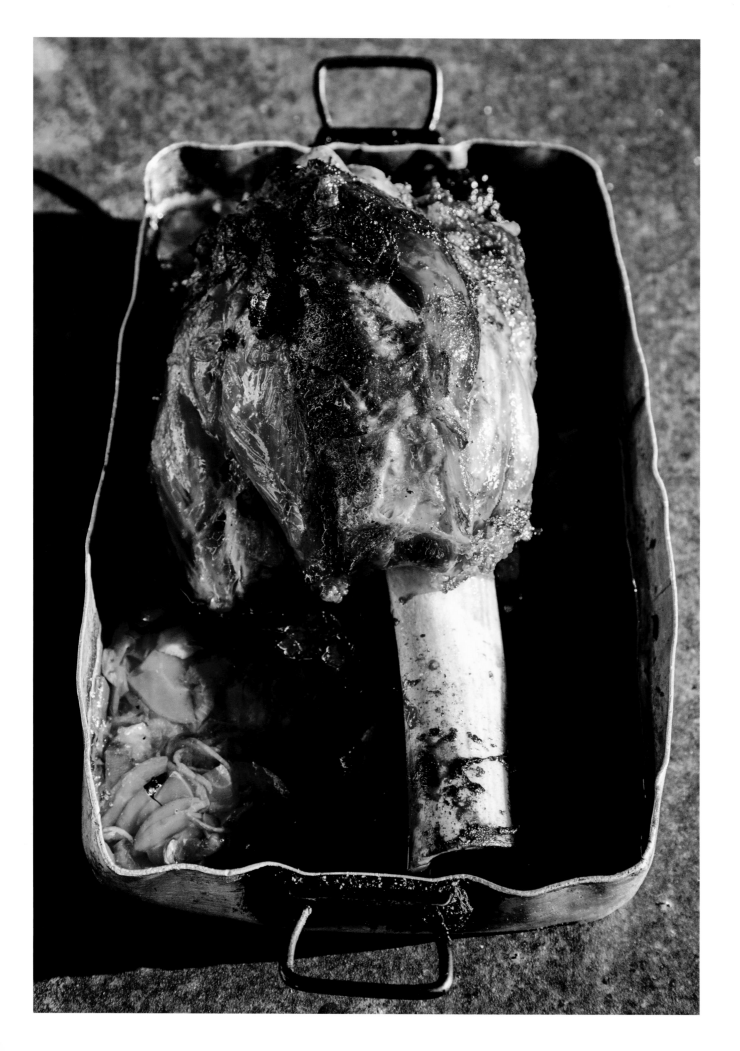

STINKO DI VITELLO
(Roasted Veal Shank)

Makes 6 to 8 servings

Stinko di vitello is the centerpiece dish of the Friulian table. It is a beautiful whole shank of veal roasted on the bone, and a very low-effort dish for a showstopper that feeds a gathering. Do not confuse stinko di vitello with its Lombardian cousin, osso bucco, which uses a cut shank. The veal can roast in the oven for several hours without drying out, so this works well as a meat or main course when you want to focus your efforts on the antipasti or the pasta. In particular, it is completely and insanely delicious with Toc' in Braide (page 75). The aroma, flavor, and, in this case, the long braise, produce an incredible base for a sauce, some of which you could reserve to make a quick pasta sauce on another occasion (see Žlikrofi with Veal Jus, page 91).

Enjoying this dish while sitting near the fireplace at La Subida is a tradition we never tire of; and because we've been visiting for more than fifteen years now, we've experimented pretty heavily with what pairs best, wine-wise. Of course, with veal shank, we gravitate toward red wine—Schioppettino, the cool-climate red of the Colli Orientali goes so well with this decadent dish, or something with more robust tannins, like a full-bodied Friulano Merlot from a producer such as Villa Russiz or Miani. Now, while *we* might focus on red wine with this vitello, don't miss the opportunity to try it with a micro-regional macerated orange wine from Oslavia. Anything from Gravner would be great with this dish.

YOU WILL NEED
Food mill, immersion blender, or stand blender

1 whole, bone-in veal shank (about 5 pounds)

Fine sea salt and freshly ground black pepper

3 tablespoons olive oil

2 medium onions, diced into ½-inch pieces

2 medium carrots, diced into ½-inch pieces

2 medium celery ribs, diced into ½-inch pieces

½ cup dry white wine

4 cups chicken stock or low-sodium chicken broth

1 bay leaf

1 rosemary sprig

2 thyme sprigs

Pinch of freshly grated nutmeg

Extra-virgin olive oil for drizzling

Preheat the oven to 350°F.

Generously season the veal with salt and pepper.

In a large Dutch oven over medium heat, warm the olive oil until almost shimmering. Add the veal shank and brown on all sides, using tongs to turn the meat—this process will take 15 minutes or so. Once nicely browned, remove the shank from the pot and set aside.

Add the onions, carrots, and celery to the pot and cook until caramelized, stirring only very occasionally to encourage the browning, 8 to 10 minutes.

Add the white wine to the pot and deglaze, scraping up any browned bits with a wooden spoon. Simmer the wine until almost evaporated, about 5 minutes, then return the veal to the pot. Pour in the chicken stock and add the bay leaf, rosemary, and thyme. Don't worry if the shank is only partially submerged. Bring to a simmer and cover.

Transfer the Dutch oven to the oven and braise for 1½ hours, basting the meat with the cooking juices every 30 minutes, until the meat starts to feel fork-tender. Turn the temperature to 300°F, uncover, and continue to cook until the meat has pulled away from one end of the bone and is very tender, another 30 minutes or so (it will happily stay tender in a low oven for longer, as needed).

Remove the meat from the pot, tent with aluminum foil, and let it rest for 20 minutes. Discard the bay leaf, rosemary, and thyme, then puree the cooked vegetables and broth using a food mill or blender. Return the puree to the pot, stir in the nutmeg, and adjust the seasoning.

Once the veal has rested, slice into portions and transfer to a platter, then spoon some of the sauce over the meat, reserving the rest to accompany alongside, and drizzle with extra-virgin olive oil. Serve immediately.

VENISON WITH PEAR, ONION, AND ZUF

Makes 4 to 6 servings

Zuf is an Italian soup or porridge often made from polenta and pumpkin or squash. The flavors go well together and make an autumn dish that can take on many forms. We like to serve zuf as a garnish or even with a Montasio cheese sauce and some grated smoked ricotta as a first course. This zuf recipe makes a delish garnish for venison, which is prepared super-simply as they do in frascas.

Note

Ask your butcher to tie the venison like a roast to round out its shape, or do it yourself! The meat should be marinated overnight, so plan accordingly.

YOU WILL NEED

Digital meat probe

6 tablespoons olive oil

1 rosemary sprig

1 thyme sprig

2 pounds venison loin or striploin, tied up like a roast

Fine sea salt and freshly ground black pepper

3 cups water

½ cup rustic polenta integrale or coarse-grind polenta (see page 72)

½ cup butternut squash or pumpkin puree

2 medium pears

1 medium red onion

¼ cup minced chives

Maldon sea salt

In a resealable plastic bag, combine 3 tablespoons of the olive oil, the rosemary, and thyme. Season the venison well with fine sea salt and pepper. Place the meat in the bag, seal, and refrigerate overnight.

In a heavy saucepan over high heat, bring the water to a boil. Slowly pour in the polenta, letting it run in thin streams through your fingers while whisking constantly to avoid any clumping. Bring the mixture to a boil, still whisking nonstop. Once the polenta starts to bubble and thicken slightly, after about 5 minutes, turn the heat to low and cover. Simmer for 1½ to 2 hours, stirring every 10 to 15 minutes, making sure to scrape the bottom and sides of the saucepan, until the polenta is fully cooked. The polenta should be extremely tender and soft.

Meanwhile, remove the venison from the marinade and insert a digital probe through one end of the meat into the center.

In a large frying pan over medium-high heat, warm the remaining 3 tablespoons olive oil. Add the venison and sear, browning it on all sides. Turn the heat to medium and continue to cook the venison until the probe registers an internal temperature of 120°F, 18 to 20 minutes. Transfer the meat to a cutting board, tent with aluminum foil, and let rest for 10 minutes—the internal temperature will climb to 135°F or so. Don't wash the pan—you'll need those juices when cooking the pears and onion.

When the polenta is fully cooked, stir in the squash puree and season with fine sea salt. Keep the zuf warm.

Core and cut the pears into six wedges each. Peel and cut the onion into six wedges.

Return the venison pan and juices to medium heat and add the pears and onion. Sauté until nicely browned and softening, 5 to 8 minutes.

Spread the minced chives on a plate. Slice the venison into ½-inch-thick pieces and roll the outside circumference of each slice in the chives.

Spoon ½ cup of the zuf onto each plate, then top with three or four slices of the venison, sprinkling the meat with some Maldon salt. Divide the pear-onion mixture among the plates and spoon alongside the meat. Serve immediately.

TIRAMISU SOUFFLÉS WITH MASCARPONE ANGLAISE

Makes 6 servings

Tiramisu is the consummate Italian dessert. And that's true in Friuli too. We didn't think you needed another tiramisu recipe, so we switched it up with this soufflé; a tender and deliberate version from Frasca pastry chef, Alberto Hernandez.

YOU WILL NEED

Six 1-cup ramekins
Microplane (optional)

CRÈME ANGLAISE

1 cup heavy cream	3 egg yolks
½ vanilla bean, seeds scraped and pod reserved	¼ cup sugar

SOUFFLÉ BASE

3 tablespoons unsalted butter, at room temperature, plus ¼ cup, cubed	1 tablespoon cornstarch
	1 tablespoon hazelnut meal (see Note, page 180)
4 tablespoons bread flour	1 shot espresso
½ cup whole milk, plus 3 tablespoons	2 teaspoons vanilla extract
	2 tablespoons coffee extract
3 eggs yolks	1 tablespoon plus 1 teaspoon coffee liqueur
2 tablespoons sugar	

Unsalted butter for brushing	½ cup mascarpone, at room temperature
Sugar for sprinkling, plus 2 tablespoons	Cacao paste for grating or cocoa powder for dusting
3 egg whites	

To make the crème anglaise: In a medium saucepan, combine the cream, vanilla seeds, and scraped pod and stir to mix. Bring to a simmer over medium heat, then remove from the heat and set aside.

In a medium bowl, whisk the egg yolks and sugar until well combined and pale in color. Discard the vanilla pod and gradually whisk the hot infused cream into the yolk-sugar mixture. Return the saucepan to low heat and stir the mixture continuously until it thickens to a custard and coats the back of a spoon, no more than 4 minutes. Strain into a bowl, lay plastic wrap directly on the surface of the anglaise, and refrigerate for up to 1 week.

To prepare the soufflé base: In a small saucepan over medium heat, melt the 3 tablespoons butter. Whisk in the bread flour, stirring to make a paste, and then turn the heat to low.

In a microwave, heat the ½ cup milk until it is hot. Whisk the milk into the flour-butter mixture and cook until it thickens. Add 1 egg yolk and stir well. Remove from the heat and whisk in the ¼ cup butter until melted and incorporated (don't worry if the mixture looks slightly curdled). Stir in the sugar, cornstarch, and hazelnut meal. Whisk in the remaining 2 egg yolks, the espresso, vanilla extract, coffee extract, and coffee liqueur, mixing well. Transfer to an airtight container and refrigerate for up to 1 week.

Brush some butter onto the bottoms and sides of six ramekins with a pastry brush, using vertical strokes along the walls. Sprinkle with sugar to coat, shaking off any excess. Refrigerate until ready to fill.

Preheat the oven to 400°F.

In a stand mixer fitted with the whisk attachment, beat the egg whites on medium speed until they form soft peaks, about 3 minutes. With the machine running, gradually add the 2 tablespoons sugar, beating for 30 to 60 seconds until firm (but not stiff) peaks form.

continued

Pour the soufflé base into a mixing bowl. Using a spatula, vigorously stir one-fourth of the egg whites into the soufflé base until well incorporated and the base has lightened up. Gently fold in the remainder of the egg whites, one-third at a time.

Place the chilled ramekins on a baking sheet. Gently divide the soufflé mixture among the ramekins, leaving ¾ inch free at the top to allow the soufflé some support in its rise. (These soufflés can be refrigerated for up to 2 hours if you're not planning on baking and serving them right away.) Transfer to the oven, lower the temperature to 375°F, and bake for 17 to 20 minutes. The soufflés are done when they have risen fully above the ramekin rim.

While the soufflés are baking, by hand, whisk the mascarpone into the crème anglaise until smooth.

As soon as the soufflés come out of the oven, use a Microplane to grate some cacao paste over the top of each, or dust with cocoa powder.

Working quickly, use a knife to gently poke a hole in the center of each soufflé to form a cavity, then pour 2 tablespoons of the mascarpone anglaise into each. Serve immediately.

FRASCA'S PEANUT BUTTER CUP

Makes 4 servings

Disclaimer: This dish is not Italian in any way, shape, or from, nor does it look like a mass-produced peanut butter cup. This dessert was, in fact, created by Frasca's very first pastry chef, Brendan Sodikoff, who is one of the most creative cooks we have ever met and is now an incredible restaurateur in Chicago. We had worked with him at the French Laundry and, having come from similar experiences in Europe, quickly became great friends. When this dish is on our menu, it sells out early every night.

Note

We achieve this dessert's signature texture using a cream whipper (the iSi Gourmet Whip Plus) charged with nitrous oxide. We outline this in the variation, but making this dessert using the analog method will be no less delicious; it just won't have the same airy texture.

YOU WILL NEED

Instant-read digital thermometer

Pint- or quart-size cream whipper (optional)

2 NO$_2$ (cream) charger canisters (optional)

⅓ cup heavy cream	2 egg whites
¾ cup coarsely chopped white chocolate	Pinch of tartaric acid
¼ cup smooth peanut butter (we use Skippy brand)	½ cup coarsely chopped peanuts
⅛ teaspoon kosher salt	2 cups chocolate gelato (see page 189)

In a small saucepan over medium-high heat, bring the cream to a boil.

In a medium bowl, combine the white chocolate, peanut butter, and salt. Pour the hot cream into the bowl and gently stir the ingredients together with a spatula until they have fully emulsified and you are left with a completely homogenous cream.

In a medium heatproof bowl set over a medium saucepan of simmering water, constantly and energetically whisk the egg whites and tartaric acid until the temperature reaches 140°F, and the eggs look like a white fluffy sponge, less

than 2 minutes. Gently fold into the lukewarm white chocolate–peanut butter cream, being sure not to overmix.

Dollop ⅓ cup of this airy ganache into each serving bowl. Over the top, sprinkle the chopped peanuts and finish with a scoop of chocolate gelato. Serve immediately.

VARIATION

Gradually whisk the egg whites into the white chocolate–peanut butter cream (no need to add the tartaric acid) until it is fully emulsified and looks rich and silky smooth. Pass through a strainer into a small saucepan and warm the mixture over low heat to between 144° and 149°F, about 4 minutes. Using a funnel or a jug with a spout, pour into a cream whipper (do not go past the max fill line). Screw on the charger holder and charge with two cream charger canisters and shake vigorously. Remove the charger holder. Angle the cream whipper head down and pipe out about ⅓ cup ganache into each serving bowl before finishing with the peanuts and gelato.

Sea

We're eating *fritto misto di mare* (fried seafood platter) in a little hut with a thatched roof on the island of Anfora in the Grado Lagoon. This is a fishing island that was once used by the Romans as a seaport for goods in transit to Aquileia; after that, it was an outpost for soldiers of the Austro-Hungarian Empire. Today, it has a small schoolhouse and some cottages, but, most important, it has Trattoria Ai Ciodi. Huts such as Ai Ciodi are called *casonis* and there are (unofficially) fifty or so in the lagoon. They began as homes for fishermen, and many still are; of the originals, a handful are open to the public as trattorias in the summer. To traverse the lagoon, you take a water taxi from Grado within the Laguna di Marano, or perhaps even a water taxi from Venice.

And water taxis are a good vantage point from which to navigate the seaside of Friuli Venezia Giulia, which we're defining here as the base of the region, namely from Latisana and below, all the way east past Monfalcone into the Carso wine region ending in one of the oldest city trading ports: Trieste. It is the reason coffee, spice, and tradeable preserves are included as recipes in this chapter. But they take a backseat to the more obvious star: the seafood of the Adriatic.

And so back to Ai Ciodi. This trattoria is the reason we visited Anfora, to eat the freshest seafood in Friuli caught an hour earlier by owner Mauro Tognon and his sons, Piero and Cristiano. In a small kitchen, they grill fresh fillet of mullet, bright coral-colored scorpion fish, whole turbot, and shrimp. Platters of spaghetti with shellfish pass our picnic table, as does *boreto* (see page 144), a fish stew in which yesterday's fresh catch is transformed into something entirely new and delicious.

Which brings up a point we kept discussing over lunch: How is it that just a short boat ride away, there are literally half a million tourists in Venice fighting over the last overpriced langoustine, while we are sitting in a casoni eating fresh seafood and drinking indigenous Malvesia wine like kings and queens? Welcome to the undiscovered magic of FVG.

A casoni trip has to be part of your Friuli seaside itinerary, as does a visit to the ancient Roman ruins in the town of Aquileia. Another way to taste the seafood of the Adriatic is to visit what we think is the best restaurant in Grado: Tavernetta all'Androna. Another one-of-a kind Friulian seafood experience can be had at Alla Dama Bianca, aka The White Lady, which sits on the peninsula just after Grado on the road to Trieste (but it's not about the setting, it's definitely about the flavor).

There are three dishes that really define Friulian seafood: *jota Triestina* (bean and pork shoulder soup from Trieste), *boreto alla Graisana* (fish soup from Grado), and *scampi alla busara* (langoustines in tomato sauce). You will find the fish soup and the langoustines in Grado or at any casoni; the jota Triestina, per its namesake, is a specialty of Trieste.

But before we venture into Trieste and its jota, let's talk about the Carso, an area just above the Adriatic but still with close proximity to the sea. One of the most peculiar and wild sceneries in all of FVG is a karst plateau for which the area is named. We've mentioned before how you might mistake a vineyard for

Caffés of Trieste

If you visit Trieste, take a walking tour of the great coffeehouses in the city where Illy coffee began. These are our must-visits.

Caffé San Marco first opened in January 1914, when Trieste was still part of the Austro-Hungarian Empire, and was popular among politically active students and intellectuals. Destroyed during the First World War by Austro-Hungarian troops, it lay abandoned for years before being reopened. When we visited on a very cold winter day, we were introduced to the new owner, who was faithfully restoring the caffè.

It is said that the interior of **Bar Torinese** (opened in 1919) on the corner of Corso Italia and Via Roma looks like a luxury liner because it was designed by a woodworker who worked on transatlantic ships. Yes, the coffee is good—but the Torinese has an even stronger cocktail hour, which is when we *highly* recommend visiting.

The splendid Piazza dell'Unità d'Italia is Europe's largest city square opening onto the sea. It is often referred to as "the living room of Trieste," being at the heart of daily public life in the city.

The **Caffè Pasticceria Pirona**, which opened in 1900, still has its original fittings and was one of the caffès frequented by writer James Joyce, who had a house on the same street from 1910 to 1912.

Having opened in 1830, **Caffè Tommaseo** is the oldest caffè in Trieste. It sits in Piazza Tommaseo, where a plaque on the outer wall declares the caffè to "the centre of the national movement from which spreads the flame of enthusiasm for Italian liberty."

a quarry in this region. The land is a mix of calcareous rock and vibrant and colorful Mediterranean vegetation, like olive trees and maritime pines. There are fortified tunnels and random trenches (and some say communication tunnels) all due to the brutal and ferocious battles that happened here during World War I.

The Carso feels different than the other regions in Friuli, and to understand it, you need to spend time here. If you do visit, we suggest you hit the vineyards of Benjamin Zidarich, Edi Kante, and Paolo Vodopivec. For lunch or dinner, be sure to stop at the roadside Locanda Devetak to experience classic dishes such as ravioli with Carso cheeses, risotto with radicchio braised in Ribolla Gialla, and (maybe) the best cotechino you've ever tasted.

From the Carso, it's about a forty-minute drive to the biggest city in Friuli, Trieste. In Trieste, you sometimes forget that you're in a major Italian city akin to Florence, Naples, or Rome—but you are. Triestinos (or Triestinis) are more reserved than their Italian compatriots. You feel this in the public square of Piazza Unità d'Italia while having an espresso at Caffè degli Specchi, just as you feel the vastness and power of what this square may have once been. During the heyday of the Austro-Hungarian Empire, Trieste was the most important merchant port, and the goods handled there came from all over Europe, the Americas, and East and West India. In that time, coffee was becoming one of the most popular goods in the world, and the city of Trieste was at the core of the trade. For that reason—and because of the Illy family's Triestino roots in the global coffee business—it has upheld its position.

It is perhaps in the province of Trieste where the frasca tradition actually began, because the first *osmiza* (meeting place) here dates back to late 1784. The local wines offered then are still the wines of today (such as Terrano, Vitovska, and Malvasia), as are the homemade specialties of cured ham, salami, *ombolo* (pork loin, very popular in the area), *ossocollo* (another pork cut), pancetta, and olives. In Trieste, the name for this food is *cucina tipica Triestino*.

The one place that absolutely does typical local Triestino food best is Trattoria da Giovanni. Big prosciutto legs hang from the ceiling, and folks from all walks of Trieste life come here. Giovanni's son, Bruno (pictured at right), is always working the slicer in this tiny gem of an *osteria* (tavern). From morning until late at night, you will find what is known as *buffet Triestino*, a constant offering of the previous mentioned specialties plus panino cotechino, fried aubergine, fresh tripe, the hearty pork and sauerkraut soup called *jota* (see page 149), and perhaps some *canederli* (dumplings, see page 213). The customers at Giovanni are a cosmopolitan crowd of adventurous eaters who are smart enough to drink local. They are Austrian, Italian, Friulian, and Slovenian . . . which is to say, they are Triestino. The countertop offerings and conviviality at Da Giovanni are the perfect microcosm of the Friulian Adriatic coast: completely singular and overwhelmingly delicious.

CRUDI MISTI
(Raw Seafood Platter)

Makes 4 servings

Crudi Misti is 100 percent *vero* (true) Friulano. From the arch of the Marche region up through Venice and Friuli, and around to Slovenia and Croatia (which is to say, any Italian land with proximity to the Adriatic), you'll come across *pesce crudo* (raw fish). The accoutrements for raw fish along the Adriatic tend to be different from sushi; pesce crudo is less adorned and more about very fresh, sublime fish sliced beautifully, served raw, and simply done up with great olive oil and salt. One of our favorite places for crudi misti is the Tavernetta all'Androna in Grado. Easy access to incredible fish and seafood is what makes coastal Friuli so special.

Hot Tip: We eat langoustines raw, which is delicious and very common in Friuli. To prepare them, simply grip the body near the head and twist. Gently pull from the shell with your thumbs and then devein if needed.

Note

Once caught, langoustines are hard to keep alive (unlike lobster), so they tend to be flash-frozen at sea. They are then sold whole or broken down and shelled for the tail meat. Look for frozen langoustines or langoustine tails at your fish market.

4 hand-dived scallops, sliced in half

4 langoustines, head and claws on, shells of body removed

4 oysters, on the half shell

Four 1-ounce slices sashimi-grade tuna

Four 1-ounce slices sashimi-grade salmon

1 lemon, cut into 4 wedges, seeds removed

Extra-virgin olive oil for drizzling

Maldon sea salt

On each plate, lay two slices of scallops, one langoustine, one oyster, one slice of tuna, and one slice of salmon. Garnish each with a lemon wedge, drizzle with extra-virgin olive oil, and sprinkle Maldon salt on everything except the oysters. Serve immediately.

WHIPPED BACCALÀ

Makes 4 servings; about 2 cups

This Italian-style dish of gently poached fish whipped with mashed potato is typical of Venice; we've enjoyed it many times over the years with a glass of Prosecco while huddled around a spread of Venetian *cicchetti* (side dishes). You occasionally come across it in FVG due to the proximity to Venice.

One night, we hosted a dinner party for our favorite winemaker friends at a beautiful villa near Rosazzo. We intentionally planned the menu around the offerings of the Saturday fishmarket in Grado, where we had come across some nice-looking salt cod. We turned it into this delicious baccalà to pair with the evening's Champagne greeting.

Note

The cod needs to be soaked in water overnight before proceeding with the recipe.

½ pound salt cod

3 garlic cloves, peeled

2 cups whole milk

1 cup cubed peeled russet potato (1-inch pieces)

⅓ cup extra-virgin olive oil, plus more for drizzling

4 slices baguette or crusty Italian bread, toasted

2 tablespoons minced fresh flat-leaf parsley

8 lemon wedges

Soak the cod in water overnight, changing the water a couple of times to remove excess salt.

The following day, drain and cut the soaked cod into 2-inch pieces.

In a saucepan over low heat, combine the cod and garlic and cover with the milk. Poach gently until the fish is cooked through and starts to flake, about 20 minutes after the milk starts to simmer. Using a slotted spoon, remove the fish pieces and set aside on a plate.

Add the potato to the milk and cook until very tender, about 25 minutes. Strain the potato, reserve the milk, and discard the garlic.

In a food processor, pulse the cod until the fish is broken up, about three pulses. Add the potato and pulse twice more. With the motor now running, gradually stream in the olive oil to form a smooth puree. If you feel the mixture is too thick for spreading generously on bread, pour in some of the reserved milk (if you find the milk too salty, use fresh milk instead) to thin out the baccalà. This will keep in an airtight container, in the refrigerator, for up to 3 days.

Spread a generous dollop of the whipped baccalà on each of the toasted bread slices. Drizzle with extra-virgin olive oil and sprinkle with the parsley. Serve with the lemon wedges.

TONNO IN SAOR

(Marinated Tuna Belly)

Makes 4 servings

Saor refers to the technique of marinating fried food in vinegar. It is a favorite conservation and preservation method that originated with Venetian fishermen and eventually made its way along the Adriatic coast into Friuli and Croatia. At Frasca, we like to add an *agrodolce* (sweet-sour) element to the vinegar by simply reducing the wine; this concentrates the sugars even further. This technique works well with tuna, but it is also fantastic with sardines and just about any fatty fish. This is the perfect seaside appetizer; serve it at room temperature on crostini with a glass of Malvasia Istriana.

¼ cup olive oil

2 garlic cloves, crushed

2 medium shallots, thinly sliced

¼ cup dry white wine

¼ cup white wine vinegar

4 black peppercorns

1 thyme sprig

½ pound tuna loin or belly, cut into 2-inch pieces

Fine sea salt

1 baguette or loaf of crusty Italian bread, sliced

4 teaspoons extra-virgin olive oil

In a heavy saucepan or sauté pan over medium heat, warm the olive oil. Add the garlic and sauté until golden brown, about 2 minutes, then add the shallots and sauté until translucent, 4 to 5 minutes more. Pour in the white wine and cook until almost completely reduced, about 2 minutes, then stir in the vinegar, peppercorns, and thyme.

Season the tuna pieces with salt, then add them to the pan. Lower the heat until you reach a bare simmer and gently poach the tuna on both sides until just cooked through, 2 to 3 minutes. Remove from the heat and let the tuna cool in the agrodolce.

Gently toast the sliced bread under a broiler or over a grill and then arrange two or three slices of the resulting crostini on each of four plates. Divide the tuna among the resulting crostini, spooning the agrodolce over the tuna. Finish by drizzling with the extra-virgin olive oil. Serve immediately.

Trieste

CAPESANTE GRATINATE

(Gratinéed Scallops)

Makes 4 servings

Bobby's wife, Danette, is Italian American, and her family hails from Abruzzo. Like many Italian Americans, Danette has grown up celebrating the Feast of the Seven Fishes every year on Christmas Eve. Even more special for their family is that Danette's father, Richard Alberico, celebrates his birthday on December 24. We started celebrating this holiday at Frasca several years ago, and it has become one of Boulder's favorite nights for families and people of all different religions.

Notes

We use the scallop shells as serving vessels.

If you can't find bay scallops (the season runs November to March), you could also butterfly (cut almost in two) larger scallops, and ask your fishmonger for some spare shells.

½ cup fresh bread crumbs

3 tablespoons minced fresh flat-leaf parsley

3 tablespoons dry white wine

3 tablespoons olive oil

2 large garlic cloves, minced

Zest of 1 lemon, plus 1 lemon, cut into wedges

2 pounds bay scallops on the shell, or 8 sea scallops, butterflied

Fine sea salt and freshly ground black pepper

Preheat the oven to broil, placing the oven rack on the second rung from the top. Line a baking sheet with crumpled aluminum foil (the foil will keep the shells from sliding around).

In a medium bowl, combine the bread crumbs, parsley, white wine, olive oil, garlic, and lemon zest and stir together. Set aside.

If using bay scallops, shuck the scallop, removing any sand and the tough outer band that holds the scallop in place (leave the coral roe, if any) and reserve the shells.

Put the scallops in the scallop shells and then place the shells on the prepared baking sheet. Top each scallop with 2 tablespoons of the crumb mixture and sprinkle with salt and pepper.

Broil for about 3 minutes, or until the scallops are cooked through and the topping is browned. Serve hot with the lemon wedges.

GRANCHIO UMIDO

(Boiled Crab)

Makes 2 servings

Visitors to the Italian coast are usually awed by the wide variety of crustaceans, mollusks, and fish offered at seaside restaurants as a matter of course; they can be fried, boiled, grilled, or battered—and served to your liking.

This dish is inspired by our love of the *granseola* crab, a type of spider crab found on the European side of the Atlantic and the Mediterranean that is especially popular in Venice, Trieste, and the surrounding coast. Here, we use the more readily available Dungeness crab, but the preparation remains the same: the crab is boiled, the meat is picked and lightly dressed and then served in the (cleaned) shell. This dish is about finding the best ingredients and preparing them simply to show off their flavors.

1 medium onion, cubed

1 bay leaf

Two 1½-pound live Dungeness crabs

Extra-virgin olive oil for drizzling

Freshly squeezed lemon juice for drizzling

1 tablespoon minced fresh flat-leaf parsley

Bring a large pot of heavily salted water to a boil. Add the onion and bay leaf and simmer for 15 minutes. Put the crabs into the pot and return to a boil, then simmer until cooked, 10 minutes more. Using tongs or a wire strainer, remove the crabs from the pot and set on a rack to cool.

When the crabs are cool enough to handle, flip one crab over so the underbelly is facing up. Remove the legs by twisting and pulling on each one. Set aside. Remove the "apron," the smaller triangular piece at the center of the underbelly, and discard. Then, separate the top shell from the underbelly by placing a finger in each of the two cavities left from the removal of the final legs and pull slowly apart. The cavity will contain mustard-brown juices and what's called "brown meat" (the darker, softly textured but strongly flavored glands in the cavity)—set that aside for now. Remove and discard the gills from the underbelly. Next, still using your hands, crack off the mouth of the crab. Crack open what's left of the belly into two pieces, and you'll see the white crabmeat poking out. Use a bamboo skewer or a seafood fork to pick the meat out of the cartilage pockets and reserve in a bowl. Keep cracking as needed to get to the final pockets of meat deep inside. Repeat with the second crab.

Now, crack the claws and legs at the joint to separate. Use the back of a chef's knife to hammer down on the side of each piece to help break it open to get at the meat inside. Spoon out the brown meat and reserve in a small bowl. Rinse out the shells until clean.

Dress the picked crabmeat with a generous drizzle of olive oil, lemon juice, and some of the brown meat, all to taste. Stir in the minced parsley.

Portion the crabmeat into the two cleaned shells. Serve immediately.

BORETO ALLA GRAISANA

(Fish Stew from Grado)

Makes 4 servings; about 1 quart

Boreto is perhaps one of the most notable classic fish dishes of Friuli, so named because it is cooked in a *boreto*, an iron casserole dish that, in the old days, was always kept on the fire. That said, it's surprisingly hard to find; your best bet is to seek it at one of the *casoni* (thatched fishing huts) that line the Grado lagoon and are only open in summer. Curiously, casoni have only one room with a fireplace, and the entrance door always faces to the west, to shelter its inhabitants from the cold Bora wind coming from the east. If you aren't arriving in Friuli by boat, you can also try this dish at our favorite Tavernetta all'Androna, in Grado.

This soup is made from a few simple ingredients typical of the lagoon: olive oil, garlic, white wine, vinegar, salt, pepper, and "waste" fish, or what could not be sold in the fishmarkets because it was poorly prized. It is typically served with white polenta that has been cooled, sliced, and then pan-seared.

Note

This stew is best when made with a mild white fish such as bass, cod, or monkfish. Its flavor relies heavily on the vinegar, so use the best-quality white wine vinegar you can find. We favor Sirk vinegar (Jŏsko Sirk makes his own at La Subida); it's made from whole Ribolla Gialla grapes rather than discarded wine, and is fermented for years in barrels. You can order it online from Gustiamo.

3 tablespoons olive oil

3 garlic cloves, crushed

2 pounds boneless mild white fish, skin-on, cut into 2-inch pieces

Fine sea salt and freshly ground black pepper

1 cup dry white wine

¼ cup white wine vinegar

2 cups fish fumet or water (both work equally well)

Crispy Fried Polenta (page 146) for serving

In a Dutch oven over medium heat, warm the olive oil. Add the garlic and cook until lightly browned, 2 to 3 minutes.

Season the fish with salt and pepper. Working in two batches, add the fish to the pan and sear until lightly browned but not cooked through, about 3 minutes. Transfer to a plate.

Turn the heat to high, pour the white wine into the Dutch oven and reduce until syrupy, about 5 minutes. Stir in the vinegar and turn the heat to low. Return the fish to the pot and cover with the reduced fish fumet. Simmer, uncovered, until the fish is tender, about 5 minutes. Transfer the fish back to the plate. Turn the heat to medium-high and reduce the broth until thickened to the consistency of a sauce, about 10 minutes—you should be left with about 1 cup of liquid. Season with salt and a generous grinding of pepper.

Warm the fish in the sauce, then transfer the fish and sauce to a shallow platter. Serve with the polenta as an accompaniment.

Crispy Fried Polenta

Makes 4 servings

If you want to make this a dairy-free dish, you can skip the butter and cheese. The butter is just for a hit of richness. At Frasca, we serve it dairy-free.

4 cups water

1 cup rustic polenta integrale or coarse-grind polenta (see page 72)

½ teaspoon fine sea salt

1 tablespoon unsalted butter (optional)

2 tablespoons freshly grated Parmigiano-Reggiano cheese (optional)

3 tablespoons olive oil

In a Dutch oven or heavy pot over medium-high heat, bring the water to a boil. Slowly pour in the polenta, letting it run in thin streams through your fingers while whisking constantly to avoid any clumping. Bring the mixture to a boil, still whisking nonstop. Once the polenta starts to bubble and thicken slightly, after about 5 minutes, add the salt and then turn the heat to low and cover. Simmer for 40 to 45 minutes, stirring well every 5 to 10 minutes, making sure to scrape the bottom and sides of the pot, until the polenta begins to come away from the sides of the pot. Stir in the butter and cheese (if using) and adjust the seasoning.

Meanwhile, lightly butter a 9 by 13-inch baking dish.

Transfer the hot polenta to the prepared baking dish. Refrigerate, uncovered, until firm, about 1 hour. Then, turn the polenta over onto a cutting board and use a sharp knife to cut it into batons or rectangles. (These will keep in an airtight container, in the refrigerator, for up to 3 days.)

In a large frying pan over medium-high heat, warm the olive oil. Add the polenta and fry until crispy on both sides, about 5 minutes total. Serve immediately.

Grado lagoon

JOTA TRIESTINA
(Bean and Pork Shoulder Soup from Trieste)

Makes 4 to 6 servings; about 2 quarts

Truly the most recognizable soup in Friuli, this hearty bean and pork shoulder soup is one of our favorite things to eat while in the region. It is mostly found in the area around Trieste and is usually a riff on sauerkraut, pork, and potatoes; it makes the perfect rustic winter soup. Here, we serve it with a garnish of brovada, turnips that are macerated in wine marc (the remains of grapes after pressing) and then fermented. It's a specialty of Friuli that accompanies roasted and boiled meats, and it makes a nice substitute for sauerkraut (a remnant of the Austrian occupation of the region, perhaps?). However, feel free to use a jar of your favorite sauerkraut instead of the brovada if you prefer.

Note

We love Marcella beans, an heirloom, thin-skinned, flat white bean named in honor of Italian cook Marcella Hazan. These are only available online from Rancho Gordo New World Specialty Food. Dry cannellini beans work well too.

1 pound pork shoulder, cut into 1-inch cubes	¼ cup chopped onion (½-inch pieces)
Fine sea salt and freshly ground black pepper	¼ cup chopped celery (½-inch pieces)
4 tablespoons olive oil	1⅓ cups dry white beans, such as Marcella beans, soaked in cold water overnight
¼ pound pancetta, cut into ¼-inch cubes	
5 garlic cloves, minced	6 cups water
¼ cup chopped carrot (½-inch pieces)	Brovada (recipe follows) for serving

Season the cubed pork with salt and pepper.

In a Dutch oven over medium heat, warm 2 tablespoons of the olive oil. Add half of the pork shoulder and sear until browned and caramelized on all sides, about 5 minutes. Transfer the meat to a plate. Add the remaining 2 tablespoons oil and the remaining pork to the pot and sear. Transfer to the plate and set aside.

In the same pot over medium heat, render the pancetta until brown and crispy, then turn the heat to medium-low, add the garlic, and gently brown, about 2 minutes. Stir in the carrot, onion, and celery and sauté, stirring regularly, for about 5 minutes. Drain the beans and add them and the pork to the pot. Cover with the water. Bring to a boil, skim off any foam, lower the heat to a simmer, and cook, uncovered, until the beans and pork are tender, about 1½ hours.

Ladle 1½ cups jota into individual bowls and top each with two spoonfuls of brovada. Serve immediately.

Brovada
Makes about 2 cups

Like a Friulian sauerkraut but simpler to make!

2 tablespoons olive oil	1 teaspoon fine sea salt
2 garlic cloves, minced	½ cup red wine
1 shallot, minced	3 tablespoons red wine vinegar
3 cups cubed turnip (½-inch cubes)	

In a medium saucepan over medium-low heat, warm the olive oil. Add the garlic and shallot and sauté until translucent, about 2 minutes. Add the turnip and salt, cover, and sweat until the turnip starts softening at the edges slightly, 4 to 5 minutes. Add the red wine, stir, and cook for 5 minutes, until most of the wine has evaporated. Add the vinegar and continue to cook until the turnips are cooked through, about 10 minutes. The brovada will keep in an airtight container, in the refrigerator, for up to 1 week.

PLJUKANCI CON RICCI DI MARE

(Handmade Pasta with Sea Urchin Sauce)

Makes 4 servings

Though pljukanci ("ply-oo-kan-see") is an Istrian hand-rolled pasta from the northernmost part of Croatia close to Friuli, this recipe comes to us via Giovanni Carta, a Sicilian chef at Le Dune, a small seafood restaurant in the town of Mariano del Friuli.

Giovanni is a portly, incredibly well-mustachioed man who moved to Friuli from Sardinia. Fair warning: Once Gio starts cooking for you, he may never stop. He'll begin with plateful after plateful of antipasti—snapper crudo, branzino crudo, bass crudo, caviar with potatoes—followed by fresh pasta with Sardinian bottarga. You think you're finished with dinner when he asks if you'd like to move along to the *secondi piatti* (second course)! When he offers a taste of his sea urchin, you have to oblige, as it is simply the best urchin preparation around.

We serve the creamy urchin sauce with pljukanci. The dough is just flour, water, and salt, and the rolling process is entirely by hand—feel free to enlist small children to help you. Easy to prepare, this is an incredibly decadent, heady dish. When perfectly emulsified with just *a little* pepper, it pairs wonderfully with a glass of Venica & Venica Malvasia.

Notes

For the sea urchin "tongues" (aka, gonads or *uni*), your fishmonger should be able to order and prepare fresh sea urchins for you (there should be five uni inside each urchin), or order a tray of prepackaged uni. Failing that, you could inquire about sourcing from a great sushi restaurant in your area. At Frasca, we buy from various purveyors along the Mendocino coast in Northern California.

This recipe will produce more sea urchin puree than you need (about 12 servings' worth), but is difficult to blend with a smaller quantity of uni. Freeze leftover puree in ice-cube trays and use as you would any bouillon cube for a seafood broth, adding 2 cups water per cube.

YOU WILL NEED
Mandoline

PLJUKANCI DOUGH

2 cups all-purpose flour, plus more as needed	1 teaspoon fine sea salt
¾ cup hot water	Semolina flour for dusting

30 sea urchin tongues (from 6 fresh sea urchins)	1 teaspoon freshly squeezed lime juice
¼ red onion	Crushed red pepper
2 tablespoons olive oil	Fine sea salt
2 tablespoons extra-virgin olive oil	

To make the dough: In the bowl of a stand mixer fitted with the dough hook attachment, combine the all-purpose flour, water, and salt and mix at low speed until a dough forms. Increase the speed to medium and knead until smooth and elastic, about 5 minutes, adding more flour as needed; the dough should feel tacky, not sticky, and be soft and pliable. Wrap in plastic and let rest for 30 minutes.

Dust a baking sheet with semolina flour.

Pinch off an almond-size piece of dough (or as small as a peanut-size piece) and roll it between the palms of your hands to extend it to 2½ inches. You can also shape the dough by rolling it with the palm of one hand on a clean kitchen surface (a very lightly oiled butcher block or wooden counter works well). The ends will be naturally tapered, resembling a miniature baguette or a young green bean. If you find the dough is sticking to your palms, wet your hands very lightly. Transfer to the prepared baking sheet. Continue to pinch and roll until you have a full tray of pljukanci. Set aside.

continued

Put the sea urchin tongues in a blender. With the motor on the slowest speed, begin to blend, adding a splash of water if necessary to achieve a smooth puree that is pourable but not too runny. Pass through a sieve and into a container. Set aside 3 tablespoons. Transfer the remaining puree to an ice-cube tray and put in the freezer. Once frozen, place the cubes in a resealable bag and store in the freezer for up to 2 months.

Bring a large pot of salted water to a boil. Line a baking sheet with paper towels.

Slice the red onion very thinly using a mandoline.

In a large sauté pan over medium heat, warm the olive oil until shimmering. Add the sliced onion and sauté until almost translucent but not limp, about 2 minutes. Transfer to the prepared baking sheet to absorb any excess oil.

Add the pasta to the boiling water and cook until tender, about 3 minutes once the water returns to a vigorous boil. Using a wire-mesh strainer, transfer the pasta directly into the sauté pan, alongside a splash of the cooking water, which will help thicken the sauce nicely as the pasta continues to absorb the water and cook in the pan. Place over high heat and stir the pasta until almost all the water has been absorbed.

Add the 3 tablespoons urchin puree and the red onion to the pan, turn the heat to medium, and stir to coat the noodles evenly. Pour in the extra-virgin olive oil, stirring well to emulsify.

Season the pasta with the lime juice, crushed red pepper, and salt and spoon into individual bowls to serve.

FUŽI WITH LOBSTER SAUCE

Makes 4 servings

Fuži is an Istrian pasta spotted on menus all along the Adriatic Sea; the farther east you go and the closer you get to Croatia and Slovenia, the more fuži you eat! This dish came to Frasca thanks to chefs Kelly Jeun and Eduardo Valle Lobo, who ran a restaurant owned by Lidia Bastianich in FVG before they moved to Boulder. Though we think of Lidia as Friulano, her roots are Istrian. This is a dish that Kelly and Eduardo learned after spending time with Lidia at her summer home in Istria. Fuži is a really simple pasta shape to make by hand—you basically roll out very thin strips of dough, cut the strips into diamonds, then wrap the dough around a dowel or the handle of a wooden spoon, and *ecco*: fuži!

Note

The lobster is pan-fried, not steamed. If you're squeamish about killing live lobsters, place them in the freezer about 30 minutes ahead of making the sauce; this renders them unconscious and easier to handle.

YOU WILL NEED

Pasta machine or stand mixer fitted with pasta attachment
Pasta cutter

FUŽI DOUGH

2 cups 00 flour (see Note, page 88) or all-purpose flour	3 tablespoons olive oil
	¼ teaspoon fine sea salt
2 eggs, beaten	Semolina flour for dusting

LOBSTER SAUCE

Two 1½-pound live lobsters	¼ cup dry white wine
¼ cup olive oil	1 cup San Marzano tomatoes, crushed
2 garlic cloves, crushed	
1 tablespoon tomato paste	Fine sea salt
2 tablespoons minced fresh flat-leaf parsley	Extra-virgin olive oil for drizzling

To make the dough: Combine the flour, eggs, olive oil, and salt according to the instructions on page 88, then roll out, continuing through step 5, and dust with semolina flour. Roll out the pasta to just under its thinnest setting, 6 or 7—you should be able to see the dusting of flour through your pasta sheet when it lies on the counter. Set aside on the prepared baking sheet and keep covered.

Using a pasta cutter, cut each sheet into long 1½-inch-wide strips. Next, cut those strips into 1½-inch squares. Brush the tip of a corner of a pasta square with water and wrap the opposite corner around a wooden spoon handle or dowel, then snugly overlap the wet tip with the dough to make a seal. Gently slip the formed fuži off the handle onto the prepared baking sheet. Repeat with the remaining squares.

Let the pasta shapes air-dry, uncovered, at room temperature for 30 to 60 minutes (or wrap in plastic and refrigerate for up to 24 hours).

continued

Bring a large pot of heavily salted water to a boil.

To make the sauce: Place one lobster, belly down, on the counter. With the blade of a chef's knife facing the head from above, plunge the knife into the body, piercing the point where the head and upper body meet the tail. Bring the blade all the way down through the head. Repeat with the second lobster.

Remove the lobster claws and twist off the knuckles. Detach the upper body from the tail and cut the upper body in half. Use a spoon to remove and discard the stomach sac, remove and discard the intestinal tract, and remove and discard the green tomalley. Cut the lobster tail at each indentation to form slices.

In a large Dutch oven over medium heat, warm the olive oil. Add the garlic and cook until lightly browned, about 1 minute. Add the lobster head pieces and sauté until caramelized. Remove the head, draining any juices back into the pan, and discard. Stir in the tomato paste and cook for 1 minute. Pour in the white wine and reduce until almost evaporated, about 1 minute. Add the tomatoes and ½ cup water and bring to a boil. Add the lobster knuckles and claws, turn the heat to low, and simmer for 7 minutes. Remove the knuckle and claws and set aside on a plate. Add the lobster tail slices to the pot and cook for 3 minutes. Remove and set aside.

Gently break off the pincher part of each claw; the meat will often stay attached to the rest of the claw and can now be slipped out (or use a seafood fork to coax it out). Return the claw meat to the simmering tomatoes and season with salt. Using your hands or a small fork or lobster pick, remove the lobster meat from the knuckles and tail shells and return to the sauce, discarding the shells.

Meanwhile, add the fuži to the boiling water and cook for 3 minutes. Use a wire-mesh strainer to remove the pasta and toss in the sauté pan to coat with the sauce. Sprinkle with the minced parsley and drizzle with extra-virgin olive oil. Serve family-style in a large shallow platter in the middle of the table.

*This spread:
Knifemaker Michael
Massaro in his Carnia
studio*

RISOTTO MARINARA

(Seafood Risotto)

Makes 4 servings

The first time we dined in Grado at the Tavernetta all'Androna, we were finishing lunch, and about to move on to dessert and coffee, when a server walked by with a dish of risotto marinara. It smelled so incredible that we decided to sit at our table for another hour until we were hungry enough to order it. The dish remains Lachlan's favorite risotto of all time and changed the way he thinks about risotto forever; essentially, he realized that risotto can sing completely on its own without butter or cheese. Wait until you taste the flavor of this magical dish. You, too, will likely be converted.

We drink Malvasia Istriana (see page 33) with this risotto. The Malvasia grape has spread all over the Adriatic and Mediterranean from its native Greece. In many places, Malvasia is a low-acid, aromatic white that we don't love with fish, but Malvasia Istriana, grown on the ponca soils, reaches great heights with pleasant orange aromatics and bracing acidity.

SEAFOOD MEDLEY

6 tablespoons olive oil	2 pounds littleneck clams, scrubbed
1 pound mussels, scrubbed	
4 garlic cloves	8 medium shrimp, peeled and deveined
6 thyme sprigs	
2 cups dry white wine	4 large sea scallops, coarsely chopped

¾ cup extra-virgin olive oil	Freshly squeezed lemon juice for seasoning
½ cup finely diced yellow onion	
1½ quarts Fish Brodo (recipe follows)	Fine sea salt
¾ cup Vialone Nano rice	¼ cup minced fresh flat-leaf parsley
½ cup dry white wine	

To prepare the seafood medley: In a large pot or Dutch oven over high heat, warm 3 tablespoons of the olive oil until shimmering. Toss in the mussels and stir gently for 30 seconds. Once the shells begin to open, add 2 of the garlic cloves, 3 of the thyme sprigs, and 1 cup of the wine. Cover and steam until all the mussels have opened, 2½ to 3 minutes. Discard any unopened mussels, then remove the opened mussels from the pot and place in the refrigerator to prevent overcooking.

In a clean large pot or Dutch oven over high heat, warm the remaining 3 tablespoons olive oil until shimmering. Toss in the clams and stir gently for 30 seconds. Once the shells begin to open, add the remaining 2 garlic cloves, 3 thyme sprigs, and 1 cup wine. Cover and steam until all the clams have opened, 5 to 8 minutes. Discard any unopened clams, then remove the opened clams from the pot and place in the refrigerator to prevent overcooking.

Once cool, remove the mussel and clam meat from their shells. (Reserve the cooking juices for another use. The broth can be strained, frozen for up to 2 months, and then warmed and emulsified with butter to make a quick sauce.)

In the bowl of a food processor, combine the cooled mussels and clams with the shrimp and scallops. Pulse four or five times to make a coarse paste. Transfer to a bowl or airtight container and refrigerate up to overnight.

In a wide heavy pot over medium-low heat, warm ½ cup of the extra-virgin olive oil. Add the onion and stir to coat. Cook, stirring often, until the onion starts to soften and become translucent, taking care not to burn it, about 5 minutes.

In a saucepan over medium heat, warm the fish brodo to a simmer, then keep warm over low heat.

continued

Stir the rice into the onion until nicely coated. Turn the heat to medium and cook until toasted—it will start to smell nutty—30 to 45 seconds. Pour in the wine and, stirring continuously, cook until the wine has almost completely evaporated, 30 to 45 seconds more. Ladle in ½ cup of the hot fish brodo, and keep stirring until the rice has absorbed almost all of it. Turn the heat to medium-low. Over the next 13 minutes, continue to add brodo to the rice, ¼ cup at a time, stirring continuously and repeating each addition as the rice absorbs the liquid fully. Keep in mind, the more you stir, the creamier your risotto will be.

After 13 minutes—this is our *al dente* moment—stir in the seafood medley along with ¼ cup brodo, turn off the heat, and let the risotto rest for 5 minutes.

Return the risotto to low heat, add a little more hot brodo to loosen as needed, and then slowly drizzle in the remaining ¼ cup olive oil, stirring nonstop. You'll notice the risotto becoming creamier as the broth and oil emulsify nicely.

Finally, season the risotto with a generous amount of lemon juice and sea salt, adjusting the consistency with any remaining brodo as needed. The consistency should be thick but somewhat loose. Fold in the minced parsley. Serve immediately in shallow bowls or family-style, in the middle of the table.

Fish Brodo
Makes about 2 quarts

Harness your inner casoni-dweller with this authentically Adriatic fish brodo.

YOU WILL NEED
Food mill

3 tablespoons olive oil	1 teaspoon cayenne pepper
4 cups diced onions	¼ cup dry white wine
1½ cups diced fennel	2 plum tomatoes, diced
2 cups ¼-inch-thick leek slices, white and tender green parts	Zest from 1 orange
1 tablespoon fennel seeds	1½ pounds fish bones, rinsed
2 teaspoons coriander seeds	2½ quarts water

In a large pot over medium heat, warm the olive oil. Add the onions, fennel, and leeks; cover; and sweat until the vegetables become slightly tender, about 3 minutes. Add the fennel seeds, coriander seeds, and cayenne and continue to cook for another 2 minutes. Add the white wine and cook until all the alcohol has evaporated.

Add the tomatoes, orange zest, and fish bones to the pot, then cover with the water and bring to a gentle simmer. Simmer for 45 minutes, remove from the heat, cover, and let rest for 20 minutes.

Using a skimmer or a slotted spoon, remove all the solids from the liquid, discarding the fish bones. Working over a bowl, run the vegetables and aromatics through a food mill, then return the puree to the pot and stir to combine.

Strain the stock through a fine-mesh sieve into an airtight container. Store in the refrigerator for up to 2 days, or in the freezer for up to 2 months.

FRITTO MISTO DI MARE

(Fried Seafood Platter)

Makes 4 servings

Most things are better when fried. What always blows me away is the variety of fish in a fritto misto in Friuli versus the typical offering in the United States. This is an opportunity to try new things and have fun with it. Fritti in Italy are *always a main course*, and not something you fill up on at the start of a meal. The fritto misto of our dreams (pictured opposite) happened at Ai Ciodi on the island of Anfora, and is well worth the boat ride through the lagoon.

YOU WILL NEED

Instant-read digital thermometer or clip-on
    deep-fry thermometer

1½ cups chickpea flour, plus more as needed	1 pound baby octopi
5 tablespoons rice flour	1½ quarts canola oil or peanut oil
Fine sea salt	3 lemons; 1 thinly sliced, 2 cut into wedges
1½ cups cold sparkling water, plus more as needed	
½ pound smelt, cleaned	
1 pound squid	

In a medium bowl, whisk together the chickpea flour, rice flour, and 1 teaspoon salt. Slowly whisk in the sparkling water. Refrigerate for 30 minutes.

Butterfly the smelt and use a sharp paring knife to remove the spine (though it can be left in and eaten, as a matter of preference). Cut the squid into 1-inch rings and leave the tentacles whole. Separate the head of each octopus from its tentacles, then cut the tentacles into pairs of two.

In a large Dutch oven over medium-high heat, warm the canola oil until it reaches 375°F. Line a baking sheet with racks or paper towels. Fill a large bowl with ice cubes and cold water to form an ice bath.

Check the consistency of your batter; it should be thick enough to coat a piece of seafood but loose enough for the excess to drip off into the bowl—you may need to stir in a splash more sparkling water or a tablespoon of chickpea flour. Place your bowl of batter over the ice bath to keep it chilled while you fry (this, and a constant oil temperature, will ensure the crispiest results).

Submerge one smelt in the batter and, using tongs or your hand, lift it from the batter, allowing the excess to drip back into the bowl; the fish should be thinly coated. Gently lower the smelt into the oil and quickly repeat with a few more fish, making sure not to overcrowd the pot, which lowers the oil temperature (adjust the heat as needed to maintain 375°F). Fry until golden, about 1 minute. Use a mesh skimmer or slotted spoon to transfer the fish to the prepared baking sheet. Lightly salt the fish while still hot. Repeat with the remaining smelt.

Next, batter and fry the squid, followed by the octopi, in the same way. Both of these will cook quickly as well, about 1 minute. Don't forget to salt them. Coat the lemon slices in batter and fry—be very careful when placing them in the hot oil; due to their water content, the oil will crackle and spit.

Transfer the crispy fish, seafood, and lemon slices to a platter. Serve immediately with the lemon wedges.

SCAMPI ALLA BUSARA

(Langoustines in Tomato Sauce)

Makes 4 servings

This dish is all about the scampi, which, contrary to North American belief, are not shrimp but langoustines. Langoustines (also known as Norwegian lobster or Dublin Bay prawns) look like crayfish but live mostly in the North Atlantic. They are thinner and smaller than lobsters, their meat is even sweeter, and the shells are an appealing, light shade of orange, which doesn't change color when cooked.

The meaning of *busara* is open to interpretation: some say it is the large iron pot that crews in Friuli use to prepare meals on their boats; others say the dish's name is derived from the word *busiara*, which means "cheating" in Trieste dialect. The latter may refer to the fact that the langoustines are somewhat hidden by the tomatoes in the sauce, or that the sauce was intended to disguise less-than-fresh fish and shellfish, making the finished product look more refined than it is.

If you really want to feel like you're eating on the coast in the salty Adriatic air, do what the Istrians do and have a cold fish starter, like Tonno in Saor (page 137), followed by this warm shellfish main.

In a large sauté pan over medium heat, warm the olive oil. Add the garlic and sauté until golden brown, 2 to 3 minutes. Add the langoustines and cook, stirring well, until opaque rather than translucent, 3 to 5 minutes. Transfer to a plate.

Add the crushed red pepper and white wine to the pan and cook for 1 minute, or until the wine has reduced by half. Stir in the tomatoes and water and bring to a simmer. Return the langoustines to the pan to reheat, another 2 to 3 minutes. Stir in the bread crumbs to thicken the sauce and then sprinkle with the parsley.

Serve the scampi on the grilled bread, drizzled with olive oil and sprinkled with salt.

¼ cup olive oil

3 garlic cloves, crushed

1½ pounds langoustines (whole, not shelled, and frozen is fine; see Note, page 134)

Generous pinch of crushed red pepper

¼ cup dry white wine

½ cup San Marzano tomatoes, crushed by hand

1 cup water

1 tablespoon fresh bread crumbs

2 tablespoons minced fresh flat-leaf parsley

1 baguette or loaf of crusty Italian bread, sliced and grilled or toasted

Extra-virgin olive oil for drizzling

Fine sea salt

CALAMARI RIPIENI

(Squid Stuffed with Dandelion Greens)

Makes 4 servings

This is a wildly simple dish to prepare that showcases the sea. When buying calamari, look for fresh and whole (intact) squid with the tentacles. You can ask your fishmonger to do the dirty work and clean them for you, but be sure you are given the bodies and tentacles.

½ cup olive oil

6 garlic cloves; 4 minced, 2 crushed

2 shallots, minced

4 anchovy fillets packed in oil

1 pound dandelion greens, coarsely chopped

1 cup vegetable stock or water

½ cup fresh bread crumbs

Fine sea salt and freshly ground black pepper

8 cleaned calamari tubes

2 cups crushed San Marzano tomatoes

Extra-virgin olive oil for drizzling

In a Dutch oven over medium-low heat, warm ¼ cup of the olive oil. Add the minced garlic and sauté until golden, about 2 minutes, then stir in the shallots and sauté until translucent, 2 minutes more. Add the anchovy fillets and stir to blend with the garlic and shallots. Stir in the chopped dandelion greens and cook until wilted, about 5 minutes. Add the vegetable stock, bring to a simmer, cover, and braise until very tender, about 25 minutes. Uncover and reduce the stock until only about 2 tablespoons remain.

Transfer the greens to a bowl to cool. Then, stir in the bread crumbs and season with salt and pepper.

Stuff the squid tubes with the dandelion mixture and transfer to a plate or small tray. Refrigerate until firm, about 20 minutes.

In a large sauté pan over medium heat, warm 2 tablespoons olive oil. Add the crushed garlic and sauté until golden brown, 2 to 3 minutes. Add the crushed tomatoes and bring to simmer, letting the juices reduce slightly, about 8 minutes. Season with salt and pepper. Set the pan aside.

In a separate frying pan over high heat, warm the remaining 2 tablespoons olive oil until almost shimmering. Working in batches, add the stuffed squid tubes and sear on one side until golden brown, about 2 minutes, then transfer into the pan with the tomato sauce, fried-side up. Place the pan over medium-low heat and simmer until heated through, about 7 minutes, then drizzle with extra-virgin olive oil. Serve family-style.

WHOLE BRANZINO IN A SALT CRUST

Makes 2 servings

As a cook who loves the bounty of the sea, Lachlan (and Bobby by extension) can never get enough of a whole roasted fish. Cooking the flesh on the bone results in one of the most succulent bites of fish you will ever taste. Baked in salt, a whole fish is tender and delicious and needs very little adornment, just a bit of great olive oil and a touch of salt; maybe pair with some fried polenta (see page 146). In Friuli, we often go out of our way to find a whole branzino, asking all of the locals from Venice to Trieste where to find the best version. The meal generally starts with crudo and ends with a whole fish. This might just be the most simple and delicious recipe in the book.

YOU WILL NEED
Instant-read digital thermometer

3 pounds kosher salt	1 garlic head, cut in half
6 egg whites	1 thyme sprig
2 lemons	Extra-virgin olive oil for drizzling
1 whole branzino (about 2 pounds), scaled and gutted	Maldon sea salt

Preheat the oven to 375°F. Line a baking sheet with parchment paper.

In a medium bowl, mix together the kosher salt and egg whites to form a paste. Spread a ¼-inch layer of the salt mixture onto the center of the prepared baking sheet. Slice one of the lemons ½ inch thick.

Place the whole fish on top of the salt, then arrange the lemon slices, garlic, and thyme inside its cavity. Spread the rest of the salt mixture over all of the fish to cover it completely.

Bake the salt-covered fish until the salt turns golden brown and the fish is cooked through, 15 to 20 minutes, or until the internal temperature of the fish reaches 135°F. Remove the fish from the oven and let it rest for 10 minutes.

Cut the remaining lemon into wedges.

Use the back of a spoon to crack open the salt crust and then discard the salt pieces. Carefully remove the fish's skin. Use a fish spatula to remove the top fillet and transfer to a plate. Lift up and discard the spine and any small pin bones. Carefully transfer the second fillet onto the plate. Drizzle with extra-virgin olive oil, sprinkle with Maldon salt, and garnish with the lemon wedges. Serve immediately.

Leaving Grado for Trattoria Ai Ciodi

GRILLED RED SNAPPER WITH SWISS CHARD AND POTATOES

Makes 4 to 6 servings

In this dish, large pieces of *pesce alla griglia* (grilled fish) are served with an array of vegetables, lemon, and simple minced parsley. This sort of eating is very common all along the coast of FVG. The vegetable accompaniments deliver a fuller experience than just cooking and eating boneless fillets. It's very simple, very Italian, very Friulano. Although red snapper tends to be easier to source, a more traditional fish for this dish is grouper (if you can get your hands on appropriate-size pieces).

YOU WILL NEED
Gas grill
2 fish spatulas or other sharp-edge spatulas
Instant-read digital thermometer (optional)

2 medium Yukon gold potatoes, cut into 1-inch dice

1 bunch Swiss chard

¼ cup minced fresh flat-leaf parsley

¼ cup extra-virgin olive oil, plus more for drizzling

Maldon sea salt

1 whole red snapper or grouper (about 3 pounds), scaled and gutted

Olive oil for rubbing, plus 3 tablespoons

Fine sea salt and freshly ground black pepper

2 garlic cloves, crushed

2 lemons, cut into wedges

Fill a large saucepan or Dutch oven with heavily salted water, add the potatoes, and bring to a boil over high heat. Turn the heat to low and simmer until the potatoes are not quite tender, about 10 minutes.

Meanwhile, separate the stems and leaves of the chard and cut both into 1-inch pieces. Add the chard to the potatoes and cook until both are very tender, 10 minutes more. Drain and set aside.

Preheat a gas grill on high, with the lid down, until very hot.

While the grill is warming up, combine the parsley with the extra-virgin olive oil and a pinch of Maldon salt to make a parsley condiment. Set aside.

Using a sharp knife, make ½-inch-deep cuts on the diagonal through the skin on both sides of the fish, every 2 inches or so—this helps the cooking and works as a handy way to check for doneness for a fish of this size. Rub the skin with olive oil, then generously season both sides, as well as the cavity, with fine sea salt and pepper.

Rub the grill's cooking surface with a paper towel that's been dipped in olive oil. Lay the fish on the grate and close the cover. Grill for 12 minutes, undisturbed, then use two fish spatulas to slowly, gradually, and gently lift the fish to turn it over—don't be afraid to gently scrape under the fish to make sure the skin is not sticking to the grill before you make the flip. Close the cover and grill on the second side until the fish flesh looks opaque and flaky and a digital thermometer registers an internal temperature of 140°F, 10 to 12 minutes. Transfer the fish to a cutting board and tent with aluminum foil.

In a large frying pan over medium heat, warm the 3 tablespoons olive oil. Add the garlic and gently brown, 2 to 3 minutes. Stir in the chard-potato mixture and season with fine sea salt and pepper. Sauté until heated through, about 3 minutes.

The spine of the fish sits down the center of the fish, from head to the tail; one fillet will be on top, the other will be on the underside. Using a sharp knife, make a vertical cut into the fish skin and flesh where the body meets the head until you can feel bone. Then, cut through the skin where the fillet meets the tail. Next, make a long horizontal cut from head to tail along the center of the fish—that's where the spine is. Use your knife or a spatula to slide the fish flesh off one side of the spinal bones. Repeat on the other side of the spine.

Pick up the tail and lift it and the spine off to reveal the fillets on the underside. Transfer the fillets to a platter and drizzle with extra-virgin olive oil and sprinkle with Maldon salt. Serve alongside the warmed Swiss chard and potatoes, with the parsley condiment and lemon wedges.

CROSTOLI WITH COFFEE MOUSSE

Makes 24 crostoli and 1 quart mousse; 12 servings

These crispy, fried treats originate from the *carnivale* celebrations in Venice, which mark the kickoff to Lent, the forty-day period leading up to Easter. With their distinctive knot in the middle, crostoli are also known as angel's wings. But you don't have to wait for Mardi Gras or Shrove Tuesday to eat these; in fact, they are now eaten year-round throughout the Veneto and Friuli (similar fried-dough treats go by other names in different regions of Italy). We've jazzed these up with a little coffee cream so you can make more of a dessert out of them. They are addictively delicious and remind us of deconstructed cannoli!

YOU WILL NEED
Instant-read digital thermometer or deep-frying thermometer
Pasta machine or stand mixer fitted with pasta attachment
Fluted pastry wheel (optional)

CROSTOLI DOUGH

2 cups all-purpose flour	1 egg, plus 2 egg yolks
1 teaspoon kosher salt	2 tablespoons plus 1 teaspoon whole milk
Finely grated zest of 1 lemon	1 tablespoon dark or light rum
Finely grated zest of 1 orange	3 tablespoons dry white wine
1 tablespoon unsalted butter, cubed	

COFFEE MOUSSE

1 cup heavy cream	½ cup sugar
1 sheet leaf gelatin	1 teaspoon kosher salt
3 egg yolks	1 cup mascarpone, at room temperature
2 shots espresso	
1 quart canola oil	Confectioners' sugar for dusting

To make the dough: In the bowl of a food processor, combine the flour, salt, lemon zest, orange zest, and butter. Pulse two or three times to blend. Add the egg and egg yolks, milk, and rum and pulse three or four times until the mixture looks sandy. Slowly pour in the wine and pulse until a dough begins to form. Remove the dough from the food processor and form into a ball shape; it will feel more pliable and tackier than pasta dough. Wrap the dough in plastic and refrigerate for 2 hours to hydrate.

To make the mousse: In the bowl of a stand mixer fitted with the whisk attachment, whip the cream on medium speed until stiff peaks form, about 2 minutes. Transfer to another bowl and set aside.

Bring a saucepan filled with 2 inches of water to a boil and then lower the heat to maintain a simmer. Fill a small bowl with water, drain but do not dry, and set aside.

Submerge the gelatin in a bowl of cold water to bloom until softened, about 5 minutes. Remove the gelatin from the water and squeeze gently to remove excess liquid. Place in prepared bowl.

In a medium heatproof bowl, whisk together the egg yolks, espresso, sugar, and salt until frothy. Place the bowl over the saucepan of simmering water (do not let the bottom of the bowl touch the water to avoid heating the egg mixture too quickly) and whisk continuously until the mixture reaches 149°F—the resulting sabayon should be thick and able to hold a ribbon (if you lift the whisk over the mixture, the batter will fall slowly, forming a ribbon that can hold its shape for a few seconds before dissolving back into the batter)—5½ to 6 minutes of whisking! The mixture will be a beautiful pale coffee color.

Transfer the coffee mixture to the cleaned bowl of the stand mixer fitted with the whisk attachment and begin whipping at medium speed. Melt the bloomed gelatin in the microwave for 5 seconds and then add to the mixer bowl, turn the speed to medium-low and continue to whisk until the gelatin is completely incorporated. Stop the machine and use a spatula to fold in the mascarpone, followed by the whipped cream. (At this point, you can transfer the mousse to an airtight container and refrigerate for up to 2 days.)

Lightly dust a work surface and baking sheet with flour. Roll out the crostoli dough into thin sheets according to the instructions on page 88, steps 2 to 5. Trim the edges and use a fluted pastry wheel or a sharp knife to cut out 2 by 7-inch strips. Gently stretch each strip of dough and tie it into a loose knot. Set aside on the prepared baking sheet.

Warm the canola oil in a heavy pot until the oil reaches 350°F. Set a wire rack on top of a baking sheet or line with paper towels.

Working in batches of four or five, add the strips of dough to the oil and fry, gently stirring them around with a wire-mesh skimmer to make sure the dough is cooking evenly on both sides, until golden brown, 2 to 3 minutes, then use the skimmer to transfer to the prepared baking sheet. (Crostoli are at their best eaten fresh, but will keep in an airtight container, at room temperature, for up to 1 day.)

Dollop ¼ cup of coffee mousse onto each plate and top with two crostoli. Using a fine-mesh sifter, lightly dust confectioners' sugar over the top. Serve immediately.

GUBANA

(Nut and Raisin Sweet Bread Roll)

Makes one 8-inch loaf; 6 to 8 servings

Gubana is a traditional Friulano yeasted sweet bread filled with a spiral of nuts and fruit. Allegedly first prepared in honor of the pope's visit to picturesque Cividale del Friuli (in the Colli Orientali) in the 1400s, this bread evolved into a traditional treat to eat at Easter and Christmas, though it's now served year-round. On one of our staff trips to Friuli, we had some time to walk around Cividale, and Scott "Scooter" Hagen, one of our front-of-house servers, took it upon himself to taste the gubana at every pastry shop in town. After proclaiming himself the "Gubana Master," he collapsed into a nap for the rest of the afternoon.

When we decided to re-create this dessert at Frasca, we worked on improving the crumb, as it always seemed a little dry. (Maybe that's why gubana is also sometimes known as "grappa cake," because grappa is typically splashed on top of each slice prior to serving.)

Our version uses a rich brioche dough; a paste of pecans, pistachios, and hazelnuts; and raisins plumped and bursting with amaro. Rather than baking the log coiled onto itself as is traditional, we cut the log into individual pieces and bake them on their sides—cinnamon-roll style!—exposing the spirals and creating a crispier, crunchier exterior. The resulting gubana is the most luscious spiced bun you'll ever try; the pieces are pull-apart perfect.

Notes

You don't need to dissolve the active dry yeast in warm water before using (unless you want proof that it's alive and active). It can simply be added along with the other dry ingredients.

The raisins need to soak in amaro for 24 hours before assembly, and the gubana dough should be refrigerated for 6 hours before proceeding, so plan accordingly.

YOU WILL NEED

Instant-read digital thermometer
2-quart container
Pizza wheel
8-inch cake pan

6 tablespoons whole milk	3 tablespoons honey
6½ cups bread flour	2 cups pecans
⅓ cup sugar, plus 1½ cups	1 cup pistachios
1 tablespoon plus 1 teaspoon active dry yeast	1 cup hazelnuts
2 teaspoons kosher salt	2 tablespoons ground cinnamon
7 eggs, at room temperature	½ teaspoon freshly grated nutmeg
1 cup unsalted butter, at room temperature, plus ½ cup melted	2 cups raisins (soaked in Amaro Nonino for 24 hours)

Using a microwave, warm the milk to approximately 104°F (but no hotter than 115°F); it should feel a little warmer than lukewarm.

In the bowl of a stand mixer fitted with the whisk attachment, on medium speed, whip together the flour, ⅓ cup sugar, yeast, and salt. Make a well in center of the bowl and add the eggs followed by the warmed milk. On the lowest setting, using the dough hook, mix until a dough starts to take shape. Stop the mixer, remove and cover the bowl with plastic wrap, and let the dough rest for 20 minutes.

While the dough rests, generously butter a 2-quart container.

On medium-low speed, resume kneading the dough, adding the 1 cup butter, 2 tablespoons or so at a time, over the course of 8 to 10 minutes, waiting for the butter to be fully incorporated before the next addition.

Turn the mixer speed to medium-high for a minute or two to ensure the dough becomes smooth and satiny. Transfer the dough to prepared container and cover tightly. Refrigerate until the dough doubles in size, about 6 hours or up to overnight.

While the dough is proofing, in a food processor, combine the honey, pecans, pistachios, hazelnuts, cinnamon, nutmeg, and remaining 1½ cups sugar and process until sandy, about 20 seconds. Transfer to an airtight container and set aside.

Generously butter an 8-inch cake pan. Lightly dust a large countertop with flour. Transfer the dough to the counter-top and work with a rolling pin until you've stretched out the dough to a thickness of ¼ inch and formed a rectangle of about 18 by 12 inches. Try to work quickly so the dough stays cool, and dust the counter with more flour as you work to prevent the dough from sticking. Trim the edges with a pizza wheel or a sharp knife, as needed, to achieve an even rectangular shape.

Lay the rectangle of dough so the long side is parallel to the edge of the counter and to you. Lightly brush with ¼ cup of the melted butter, then spread the ground nuts and spices into a thin layer covering all of the dough. Next, drain the raisins (but don't squeeze them) and sprinkle evenly over the top. Roll up the dough to form an 18-inch log, then use a large serrated knife to cut the log into six or seven 3-inch-wide pieces.

Arrange the cut rolls sideways in the prepared cake pan, placing one in the center and the others around it, at an equal distance. The pieces will all be gently touching at this stage.

Preheat the oven to 350°F.

Place the cake pan in a warm, humid place to proof for 45 minutes, or until the rolls have filled out and started to rise to about the edge of the cake pan. (A microwave containing a Pyrex jug of just-boiled water makes a great proofing box!) Once the rolls have risen above the sides of the pan, use sharp scissors to make a 1-inch-deep cut across the entire top of each roll.

Bake the rolls for 25 minutes, then rotate the cake pan, increase the temperature to 400°F, and bake until the tops are a deep golden brown, about 15 minutes more.

Remove the pan from the oven and immediately brush with the remaining ¼ cup melted butter.

Let the rolls cool for 10 minutes, remove from the pan, and transfer to a cooling rack. (The rolls will keep in an airtight container, at room temperature, for up to 3 days.)

Serve once completely cool—each roll will pull apart by hand, or you can cut into the cake to make more portions.

POLENTA CAKE

Makes one 9 by 13-inch cake; 12 servings

Polenta is one of the most recognizable elements in many savory Friulano dishes. But we wondered why there are no sweet versions of this mainstay and set out to make one ourselves. Where we landed—after much trial and error— is this incredibly moist and greatly textured sweet and somewhat surprising dessert (which also makes a satisfying midafternoon snack). This may remind you of a French frangipane, but rather than almond, you really taste the cornmeal, which is enriched by the hazelnut. Once placed to cool on the kitchen counter, this rich (and gluten-free!) cake never stays around very long. And the yogurt gelato adds a refreshing tang.

Notes

We like to use blue Moretti Bianca white cornmeal in this cake, but any medium-ground cornmeal will work.

To make your own hazelnut meal, pulse 2 cups raw hazelnuts in a food processor until finely ground. Store in an airtight container, in the refrigerator, for up to 1 week.

YOU WILL NEED
9 by 13-inch baking dish

1 cup unsalted butter, at room temperature	2 teaspoons kosher salt
1 cup sugar	Finely grated zest of 2 lemons
3 eggs	2 tablespoons minced fresh rosemary
¾ cup medium-ground cornmeal	12 sage leaves
1 cup hazelnut meal (see Note)	Yogurt Gelato (page 186) for serving
1½ teaspoons baking powder	Berry Sage Coulis (facing page) for serving

Preheat the oven to 325°F. Grease a 9 by 13-inch baking dish.

In a stand mixer fitted with the whisk attachment, on low speed, cream the butter and sugar until pale and light, about 3 minutes. Add the eggs, one at a time, taking care to make sure they are combined before each addition (you might have to stop the machine and scrape down the sides and bottom with a spatula).

In a separate bowl, whisk together the cornmeal, hazelnut meal, baking powder, and salt. Add half of this dry mixture to the butter mixture on low speed, then add the lemon zest, the other half of the dry mixture, and the rosemary, being sure to stop the mixer to scrape down the sides and bottom of your bowl so that all the ingredients are incorporated evenly. Transfer the mixture to the prepared pan.

Bake the cake until it is set and a cake tester comes out clean, 30 to 40 minutes. Once done, let the cake cool for 60 minutes. (The cake will keep in an airtight container, at room temperature, for up to 3 days.)

Place a square of cake on each plate, lay a sage leaf next to each slice, scoop a nice quenelle of gelato on top of the sage leaf, then ladle a spoonful or two of coulis over the gelato. Serve immediately.

Berry Sage Coulis

Makes about ⅔ cup

YOU WILL NEED

Immersion blender (optional)

10 raspberries

6 blackberries

4 strawberries, hulled and
coarsely chopped

¼ cup sugar

1 large fresh sage leaf

In a small saucepan over low heat, combine the raspberries, blackberries, strawberries, and sugar. Cook, stirring often to break up the berries, until they have softened completely, about 30 minutes. Remove the pan from the heat and add the sage leaf, stirring vigorously to release its oils into the coulis, then discard the sage leaf. If you find the coulis too chunky for your liking, you can puree half the mixture using an immersion blender and stir it back into the coulis. Transfer to an airtight container and store in the refrigerator for up to 3 days.

CHOCOLATE SEMIFREDDO WITH RASPBERRY COULIS

Makes 6 servings

With this recipe, we're going to pull back the curtain on creating a cookbook: Most of the dishes in this book have been in our arsenal for the last decade in one form or another. The yellow, lined, loose sheets of paper on which the recipes are written are coffee-stained and used again and again in our kitchen. But a couple of the recipes you see in these pages were written specifically *for* this book. They are simple Italian classics that we have wanted to serve in the restaurant but haven't gotten around to developing . . . until now!

This dessert is a partly frozen chocolate *semifreddo* (ice cream) dome that sits on a chocolate-hazelnut cake base, topped with raspberry coulis—essentially, a fancy ice-cream treat. It's a dessert you can eat at a white-tablecloth restaurant, or at the beach using your hands.

YOU WILL NEED

Six 3-inch ramekins or small bowls

9 by 13-inch baking dish

Offset spatula

3-inch cookie cutter

CHOCOLATE SEMIFREDDO

½ cup heavy cream	2 teaspoons cacao paste (optional)
½ cup milk chocolate fèves (discs or wafers)	Pinch of kosher salt
5 egg yolks	½ cup sugar
¼ teaspoon vanilla bean paste	⅓ cup water

CHOCOLATE-HAZELNUT CAKE

⅔ cup dark chocolate fèves (discs or wafers)	Pinch of kosher salt
½ cup unsalted butter, at room temperature	2 eggs, separated
½ cup sugar	1 cup hazelnut meal (see Note, page 180)

RASPBERRY COULIS

2 cups fresh or frozen raspberries	2 tablespoons sugar
2 tablespoons red wine vinegar	2 tablespoons light corn syrup
Finely grated zest and juice of 1 lemon	½ teaspoon kosher salt

To make the semifreddo: In the bowl of a stand mixer fitted with the whisk attachment, on medium speed, whip the cream until stiff peaks form, about 2 minutes, then transfer to another bowl and set aside in the refrigerator.

In a heatproof bowl over a saucepan of simmering water (make sure the bottom of the bowl doesn't touch the water), regularly stir the milk chocolate until melted, about 2 minutes. Alternatively, microwave the chocolate in short 10- to 15-second bursts, stirring well after every burst, until completely melted. Set the melted chocolate aside.

In the cleaned bowl of the stand mixer fitted with the whisk attachment, combine the egg yolks, vanilla paste, cacao paste (if using), and salt. Whip on medium-high speed until the mixture is pale yellow, thick, and can form a ribbon (if you lift the whisk over the mixture, the batter will fall slowly, forming a ribbon that can hold its shape for a few seconds before dissolving back into the batter), about 4 minutes.

In a small saucepan over high heat, combine the sugar and water and bring to boil. When the sugar has reached a boil, with the mixer running on medium-high speed, slowly stream the hot sugar syrup down the side of the bowl and into the egg yolk mixture. Turn the speed to high and whip until the mixture has started to cool, 5 to 6 minutes. Turn the speed to medium and stream in the melted chocolate to combine. Stop the mixer and use a spatula to fold in the whipped cream and then freeze for at least 4 hours or up to 2 days.

To make the cake: Meanwhile, in a heatproof bowl over a saucepan of simmering water (make sure the bottom of the bowl doesn't touch the water), regularly stir the dark chocolate until melted, about 2 minutes. Alternatively, microwave the chocolate in short 10- to 15-second bursts, stirring well after every burst, until completely melted. Set the melted chocolate aside.

Preheat the oven to 325°F. Butter a 9 by 13-inch baking dish and then line with parchment paper.

In the bowl of the stand mixer fitted with the paddle attachment, on medium speed, cream the butter, sugar, and salt until well combined. Add the egg yolks one at a time, beating well after each addition. Stream in the melted chocolate, being sure to stop the mixer to scrape down the sides and bottom of your bowl so that all your ingredients are incorporated evenly. Add the hazelnut meal and mix on low speed until combined. Transfer the cake batter to another bowl.

In the cleaned bowl of the stand mixer fitted with the whisk attachment, on medium speed, whip the egg whites to medium-stiff peaks, about 4 minutes. Vigorously stir one-fourth of the egg whites into the cake batter to lighten it, then gently fold in the rest of the egg whites, one-third at a time. Spread the batter in the prepared baking dish and use an offset spatula to smooth the top.

Bake the cake until it is just firm to the touch and a cake tester comes out clean, about 17 minutes. Transfer to a wire rack to cool in the pan, about 20 minutes, then transfer to a cutting board and, using a 3-inch cookie cutter, cut out six circles and set aside in an airtight container, at room temperature, for up to 3 days.

To make the coulis: In a small saucepan over medium-low heat, combine the raspberries, vinegar, and lemon zest and juice. In a separate bowl, whisk together the sugar, corn syrup, and salt, then add to the saucepan and stir to combine. Cook the raspberry mixture until the raspberries have broken apart, about 5 minutes. Let cool. (The coulis will keep an airtight container, in the refrigerator, for up to 3 days.)

Unmold the semifreddos onto a tray, peel off the plastic wrap, and use an offset spatula to place each semifreddo dome on top of a chocolate-hazelnut cake circle. Let sit at room temperature for 15 minutes. Transfer to individual plates and spoon the raspberry coulis over top of each. Serve immediately.

GELATI

Each month, we change the gelato flavors on the Frasca menu. If you multiply the number of monthly gelati by the number of years we have been open, you get a lot of gelato. And so, we're hoarding a lot of gelato recipes—stuffed in the walk-in freezers, in our pastry chef Alberto's apron, and even on Bobby's desk (our daily gelato-tester extraordinaire). So many! We only wanted to include the hits, so we chose three that work well with all of the desserts in this book, and, if we do say so, are excellent recipes.

Note

You may be surprised to find ice-cream stabilizer, glucose and dextrose powders, or liquid invert sugar in the ingredients lists, but using them is a classic restaurant trick that helps make the gelato extra-smooth and easier to scoop from a cold state. All can be purchased online.

Yogurt Gelato

Makes about 1¼ quarts

We love this recipe because it's not wearing any makeup. For us, the ideal spoonful of yogurt tastes clean with a milky-sweet flavor and has a mild but definite tang. You know when frozen yogurt thaws and that slight hint of sour is illuminated? This gelato has that element.

Thirteen years ago, during our second staff trip to Friuli, we had yogurt gelato at Terre e Vino, a favorite osteria. It was served with cooked berries atop. Another favorite gelateria, OG Gelato, is right next door to our favorite wine bar in Friuli, Al Cappello in Udine. All are worth a visit.

YOU WILL NEED
Instant-read digital thermometer
Sieve
Ice-cream maker (remember to freeze its bowl
    well ahead of time!)
8½ by 4½-inch loaf pan

1 cup sugar	2 cups whole milk
Scant 1 cup glucose powder (see Note, page 185)	⅔ cup heavy cream
	2 cups plain full-fat yogurt
1 teaspoon ice-cream stabilizer (see Note, page 185; optional)	⅔ cup buttermilk

In a heavy saucepan, whisk together the sugar, glucose powder, and ice-cream stabilizer (if using). Stir in the milk and cream, place over medium heat, and cook, stirring often, until the resulting mixture reaches 175°F on a thermometer, 5 to 6 minutes; it will thicken and bubble around the edges.

Meanwhile, fill a large bowl with ice cubes and cold water to form an ice bath and then set a medium bowl on top.

Remove the pan from the heat and strain the milk-cream mixture through a sieve into the bowl set over the ice bath. Stir a few times to speed up the cooling.

In another large bowl, combine the yogurt and buttermilk, then stir in about one-fifth of the cooled milk-cream mixture, whisking to remove any lumps. Add the remaining milk-cream mixture and whisk this ice-cream base well.

Pour the base into the bowl of an ice-cream maker and churn, according to the manufacturer's instructions, until the base feels cold and has started to thicken, 25 to 30 minutes. Transfer the soft gelato to a loaf pan (or an airtight container of your choice), wrap tightly in plastic, and freeze for 2 hours before serving. The gelato will keep, in the freezer, for up to 1 month.

Custard Gelato
Makes about 1 quart

We'll concede that FVG isn't a big dessert destination. You won't find the *sfogliatelle* (puffs) of Naples, the cannoli of Sicily, tortas from Capri, Tuscan biscotti, or Monte Biancos from the Dolomites. But this is Italy after all, so what you *will* find is gelato. Combine this with FVG's historical ties and proximity to Austria, and you have some of the finest Vienna-inspired custards in the world.

At Frasca, we take the mellow yet nuanced custard flavor of a simple crème brûlée and make it into a very smooth, decadent gelato that goes with just about anything. This recipe also serves as a great base for other flavors such as vanilla bean, mint, espresso, or fennel pollen.

Note

This recipe calls for a lot of egg yolks. Leftover egg whites can be refrigerated for up to a week, but if using in a Pavlova or meringue, or for soufflés, they should be at their freshest.

YOU WILL NEED

Instant-read digital thermometer
Sieve
Ice-cream maker (remember to freeze its bowl
     well ahead of time!)
8½ by 4½-inch loaf pan

2¾ cups whole milk	1 tablespoon dextrose (see Note, page 185)
1 cup plus 2 tablespoons heavy cream	¼ teaspoon ice-cream stabilizer (see Note, page 185)
¾ cup sugar	2 tablespoons liquid invert sugar (see Note, page 185)
1 cup (about 12) egg yolks	
1 teaspoon kosher salt	

In a heavy saucepan over medium heat, bring the milk and cream to scalding.

In a mixing bowl, vigorously whisk together the sugar and egg yolks until the mixture takes on a pale yellow color, about 3 minutes. Once the mixture holds a ribbon (if you lift the whisk, the batter will fall slowly, forming a ribbon that can hold its shape for a few seconds before dissolving back into the batter), whisk in the salt, dextrose, ice-cream stabilizer, and invert sugar.

Fill a large bowl with ice cubes and cold water to form an ice bath and then set a medium bowl on top.

Pour a little of the hot milk-cream mixture into the yolk mixture to temper, combine both mixtures in the saucepan, turn the heat to medium-low, and cook, stirring regularly. Once you see the mixture start to thicken a little, place an instant-read thermometer in this custard and continue cooking and stirring until the thermometer registers 180°F, 5 to 7 minutes. Remove the pan from the heat and strain the custard through a sieve into the bowl set over the ice bath. Stir this ice-cream base a few times to speed up cooling.

Pour the base into the bowl of an ice-cream maker and churn, according to the manufacturer's instructions, until the base feels cold and has started to thicken, 25 to 30 minutes. Transfer the soft gelato to a loaf pan (or an airtight container of your choice), wrap tightly in plastic, and freeze for 2 hours before serving. The gelato will keep, in the freezer, for up to 1 month.

Varitations

To experiment with adding flavor to this gelato, try one of the following: infuse 1 tablespoon dried lavender in the hot milk-cream mixture (then strain); when whisking in the invert sugar, add 1 tablespoon coffee extract or a few drops of peppermint extract; or stir in some chopped cookies after pouring the cool base into the bowl of the ice-cream maker, for a cookies-and-cream gelato. In fact, you can play around with any flavor of your choice!

Trieste

Chocolate Gelato

Makes about 1¼ quarts

If you are a chocolate lover, this may be the game-changing bite of your life when it comes to chocolate ice cream. *Decadent* is an understatement. The fat content and mouthfeel of this gelato are as over the top as the flavor. This is the gelato that everyone fights over.

Note

This recipe does not call for glucose powder, stabilizer, or invert sugar like the yogurt and custard gelatos. That's because the fat content in the chocolate does the ratio and texture work for us, so no need for any secret weapons.

YOU WILL NEED

Instant-read digital thermometer
Sieve
Immersion blender
Ice-cream maker (remember to freeze its bowl
    well ahead of time!)
8½ by 4½-inch loaf pan

1 cup chopped dark chocolate (at least 66% cocoa solids)

2½ cups whole milk

½ cup heavy cream

3 egg yolks

1 cup sugar

1 tablespoon plus 1 teaspoon cocoa powder

1 teaspoon kosher salt

Place the chopped chocolate in a bowl with tall sides. Fill a separate large bowl with ice cubes and cold water to form an ice bath.

In a heavy saucepan over medium heat, bring the milk and cream to scalding.

Meanwhile, in a medium bowl, whisk together the egg yolks, sugar, cocoa powder, and salt until well combined, about 2 minutes. Pour a little of the hot milk-cream mixture into the yolk mixture to temper, combine both mixtures in the saucepan, turn the heat to medium-low, and cook, stirring regularly. Once you see the mixture start to thicken a little, place an instant-read thermometer into this custard and continue cooking and stirring until the thermometer registers 180°F, 5 to 7 minutes. Remove the pan from the heat and strain the custard through a sieve into the bowl containing the chocolate. Using an immersion blender, emulsify the hot custard and chocolate until well combined. Transfer the bowl to the ice bath and regularly stir this ice-cream base to cool completely.

Pour the base into the bowl of an ice-cream maker and churn, according to the manufacturer's instructions, until the base feels cold and has started to thicken, 25 to 30 minutes. Transfer the soft gelato to a loaf pan (or an airtight container of your choice), wrap tightly in plastic, and freeze for 2 hours before serving. The gelato will keep, in the freezer, for up to 1 month.

Mountains

When we speak of the mountain region of Friuli, we mean Carnia. A continuation of Europe's Central Alps, this range is called the *Alpi Carniche* (Carnic Alps) in Friuli; once it crosses east into Slovenia, it becomes the *Alpi Giulie* (Julian Alps). Similar to its towering Dolomite cousins to the west, these mountains have been chiseled out of limestone and stood the test of millenniums. But unlike the sunny and snow-covered peaks of Cortina d'Ampezzo in the southern Dolomites, these peaks, and the towns nestled within them, have always been—and continue to be—cloaked in mystery.

Unless you have a direct tie to this region, you've probably not heard of the village of Tolmezzo; the medieval town of Venzone; or the towns of Arta Terme, Maniago, Sauris, and Tarvisio. There are ancient cultures, people, and ingredients hidden deep among the crags and beyond the generations. A landscape of century-old decrepit castles built onto rocky pre-Alps, as the sun fades and the shadows begin to creep, Carnia can feel like a sort of Italian Transylvania.

"I still remember the first time Lachlan and I went to Sauris," as Bobby tells it. "We drove there from Cormons, not knowing what to expect. It really seemed as if everyone was staring at us like we were aliens. We stayed at a small inn, and every morning the men would come into the inn's restaurant to do a shot of grappa before going out to work, while the women would stack firewood. These were probably the most fearless and strong women we have ever come across." The local dialect in Sauris, called Saurano, is Germanic, as the town was founded by Germans in the fourteenth century. Most people here are trilingual, speaking Friulano, Saurano, and Italian; how is that for niche?

Breathtakingly beautiful and wild, for centuries, Sauris could only be reached via a steep path; it sits at just under 4,000 feet elevation. There wasn't a paved road in Sauris until 1968; and rumor has it that during WWI, no one in Sauris even knew the war was happening. The isolation of towns such as Sauris is common in Carnia, and this defines the region's singularity; you are in the center of Europe, yet all alone. Unlike southern Italy, where you will be embraced within minutes, Carnians are more reserved, like their Austrian neighbors. But once they do warm up, you have a friend for life.

We experienced this when we stayed in the village of Ovaro (population approximately 1,800) at the base of Monte Zoncolan—perhaps the landmark for which this region is most famous thanks to the *Giro d'Italia* cycling race. While in Ovaro, we cooked for weeks with our neighbors in an attempt to refamiliarize ourselves with the typical local ingredients so we could come back to Frasca with fresh menu inspiration. It was a revelation! Pork in all forms, especially the beechwood-smoked prosciutto and speck from our favorite mountain ham producer Wolf (in Sauris), was on tap. Wild mushrooms and potent garlic, horseradish, root vegetables, and cabbage straight from the garden; apples and other orchard fruit; and spices such as poppy seeds, cinnamon, and caraway are permanent fixtures in the Carnian pantry.

In the recipes that follow, two cheeses play big as well: *ricotta affumicata* (smoked ricotta) and Montasio. The smoking of the ricotta is a familiar story for those who know Alpine meats and cheeses. It is a tradition that began when

Carnia's earliest dairy farmers produced more ricotta than their families could eat within the season. And so, they smoked and cured the cheese over *fogolâr* (open fire), which was an excellent method of preservation that imparted a truly unique smoky flavor. And like any old-world terroir, pairing this cheese is by design *meant* for its local contemporaries; as a sauce, it elevates squash gnocchi (see page 218) and adds a completely different depth to savory *cjalsòns* (see page 225)—which are themselves the quintessential Carnian dish.

And then there is, of course, Montasio. Friuli's king of cheese is named after the tallest massif: Montasio. It's here on the Alpine pastures that, from the earliest days, Benedictine monks began collecting cow's milk and sending it to all parts of Friuli. And the cheese is still produced here today. We visited Malga Montasio on an early spring day when the dairy was in full swing producing *fresco* (aged 2 months), *mezzano* (aged 5 to 10 months), and *stagionato* (aged more than 10 months). The cheese is white in color to begin, but as it ripens, it picks up a yellow hue and distinct tang. A reminder to frico fans: the best age for Montasio is 6 months or less for Frico Caldo (page 70), and 1 year or more (*"vecchio"*) for Frico Croccante (page 71).

The difference between this *malga*, and say, an *alpage* in the French Alps (both high-mountain pastures), is its vastness and, yes, its isolation even compared to other high-altitude dairies. To be true Montasio, legally, this cheese must be produced in Friuli Venezia Giulia, or certain provinces of the Veneto. It is a certified DOP (a designation of origin) protected by the European Union and can be authenticated by the stamp on its rind.

The mountainous region of Friuli may be more humble than its wine region counterpart but it is deeply rich in history *and* food culture, as the following recipes for authentic dumplings (*cjalsòns* and *canederli*), smoked ricotta, succulent meats, and mountainous-inspired mushrooms and garlic can attest. In a way, its unassuming demeanor has worked in favor of authenticity, as you simply do not see tourists here. Like a matryoshka doll, Friuli is the undiscovered region of Italy, and Carnia is the undiscovered region within Friuli. The really crazy part is that it's less than eighty kilometers from the heart of the Carnic Alps to downtown Udine. You could be having a coffee at Caffè Beltrame after viewing a painting by FVG artist Afro Basaldella, and an hour later be on a completely different, elevated plane. Two of our favorite restaurants in Friuli are located in the mountains: Ristorante Laite is in the town of Sappada and has an incredible Friulano wine list. There is also Ristorante alla Pace in Sauris, an eleven-seater that was founded in 1804. Both of these gems work with local ingredients and have a deft touch with foraging. We have taken our staff to both, and the journey to arrive at each takes determination and focused driving through serpentine tunnels. After many courses and bottles, let's just say that eight years later, some of our staff are still recovering from the drive back.

A herdsman on Monte Zocolan

RAFANO

(Creamed Horseradish and Apple)

Makes about 2 cups

Rafano is Italian for "horseradish," which is very close to the French word for horseradish, *raifort*. A root vegetable known for its ability to clear the sinuses, horseradish can be found all over the mountains of Alto-Adige in northern Italy, as well as in Friuli's Carnic Alps (where it is sometimes referred to as *cren*).

Eating in the mountains can be meat-and-cheese heavy, so we love to saber this tart and crunchy condiment through our high daily intake of speck and prosciutto when we're traveling in Friuli. Our favorite cured-meat producer, Wolf, located high up in the village of Sauris, makes a delicious version. Packing a jar of rafano along with salumi, some aged Montasio, a crusty loaf of bread, and fig jam makes a winning knapsack lunch after cycling up the Monte Zoncolan.

1 cup crème fraîche

½ cup peeled and grated horseradish

½ Granny Smith apple, coarsely grated

½ teaspoon fine sea salt

In a small bowl, combine the crème fraîche, horseradish, apple, and salt and mix well. Transfer to an airtight container or a glass jar and refrigerate for 30 minutes before using. This condiment will keep, in the refrigerator, for up to 3 days.

WILD MUSHROOM AND MONTASIO FONDUTA

Makes 4 servings

Montasio, a creamy, semifirm mountain cheese, derives its name from the Montasio mountain range in Friuli's northeast corner. For this recipe, we were inspired by the Malga Montasio dairy farm on the *Altiplano del Montasio* (Montasio plateau) and by the surrounding woods that were sprouting wild mushrooms. Here, the Montasio is grated and cooked to form a bowl for wild mushrooms and Montasio fonduta. It's essentially an edible basket made of Montasio . . . full of more Montasio.

Note

Montasio cheese is available at all fine Italian purveyors but can also be ordered online. Use a mix of wild and farmed mushrooms of your choosing; for example, chanterelles, morels, black trumpet, hen of the woods, nebrodini, or shiitake.

YOU WILL NEED

Small heatproof bowl, about 3 inches wide at the base
Small offset spatula

POLENTA-MONTASIO BASKET

½ cup rustic polenta integrale or coarse-grind polenta (see page 72)	½ cup very finely grated Parmigiano-Reggiano cheese
1 cup finely grated Montasio cheese	

FONDUTA

2 tablespoons unsalted butter	2 cups grated Montasio cheese
2 tablespoons all-purpose flour	Fine sea salt
1½ cups whole milk	

MUSHROOMS

2 tablespoons olive oil	Fine sea salt
2 cups assorted wild mushrooms (or use domestic such as shiitake, hen of the woods, nebrodini)	2 medium shallots, minced
	2 tablespoons minced fresh chives

Minced fresh chives for sprinkling

To make the basket: In a large bowl, combine the polenta, Montasio, and Parmigiano.

Set a wire rack and a small bowl, upside down, next to your stove top. Warm a nonstick frying pan over medium heat.

Give a good stir to the polenta-cheese mixture to evenly redistribute the polenta, which may have settled to the bottom of the bowl. Scoop up ½ cup of the mixture and sprinkle gently into the center of the preheated pan. Use a small offset spatula or the back of a spoon to spread the

continued

mixture into a thin circle measuring 6 to 7 inches in diameter. It's okay if the edges are a little shaggy or uneven (it will make the final shape of the basket more appealing).

Let the cheese sit until it starts to melt and has formed a crust, about 2 minutes. Using a spatula or two, gently flip over and cook the other side, another 2 minutes. With the spatula, pick up the cheese disk and transfer to the top of the upside-down bowl (don't turn the disk over, the prettier texture will be on the side now hugging the bowl). Gently press down on the sides to shape the cheese crust around the bowl (you may need to use a kitchen towel if the cheese feels too hot to handle). Let cool for 2 to 3 minutes (during which time you can start frying the next basket). Carefully lift the cooled cheese basket and transfer, right-side up, to the rack.

Repeat the portioning and cooking of the cheese-polenta mixture to make another three baskets. Set aside.

To make the fonduta: In a heavy saucepan over medium-low heat, melt the butter. Whisk in the flour and cook for 2 to 3 minutes, whisking regularly until combined and starting to color.

In a saucepan over medium-high heat or in the microwave, bring the milk to scalding. Stream the hot milk into the butter-flour mixture, whisking vigorously to avoid any lumps. Stir in the Montasio and whisk until fully melted. Season with salt. Keep warm over very low heat.

To prepare the mushrooms: In a large frying pan over medium-high heat, warm the olive oil. Spread out the mushrooms in the pan and season with salt. Let sit for 2 minutes, then toss once and stir in the shallots. Sauté until the mushrooms are fully cooked and wilted, about 5 minutes. Remove from the heat and stir in the 2 tablespoons chives.

Place a polenta-cheese basket in each of four shallow serving bowls. Spoon the fonduta into the bottom of each basket to cover, then top with one-fourth of the sautéed mushrooms, followed by more fonduta. Sprinkle the minced chives over the tops. Serve immediately.

The Alpe-Adria Cycling Path

We came across this cycling path after visiting the Malga Montasio. Being cyclists ourselves, we heard through the grapevine about a nearby abandoned train station called Chuisaforte that had been converted to a snackbar and reststop for those riding the path. We stopped and were blown away to realize that a 410-kilometer designated cross-border cycling path had been built alongside the old, unused railway line. The path begins in Salzburg, Austria, and continues through the Gastein Valley before cyclists have to board a train for a short distance through Carinthia. The cycling resumes in Villach, Austria, where the path crosses over the border and into FVG. From there it descends from the Carnia all the way to Udine.

If you want to cycle the Friuli section, we suggest dividing the trip into three days: beginning in Tarvisio, sleeping in Venzone and Udine, and then finishing in Grado. This is an unbelievable way to see and feel the terroir of Friuli across all three landscapes.

FRITTATA WITH MOUNTAIN HERBS

Makes 6 servings

This recipe makes a great simple lunch or afternoon snack in Friuli. It's so popular, in fact, that you'll be able to pick up a packaged "frittata herb mix" at any fresh produce seller. Restaurants buy it, and you even see the packets of dried herbs in farmers' markets. After a long ride over a mountain, we love to have this frittata as a recovery snack. The formula is simple: two eggs per person, whipped with a fork, and lots of minced fresh herbs.

Nicola Manferrari at Borgo del Tiglio winery loves his Friulano wine with eggs, and we have to agree. Ditto to Doro Princic's Pinot Bianco and eggs.

12 eggs

1 tablespoon minced fresh mint

1 tablespoon minced fresh flat-leaf parsley

1 tablespoon minced fresh chervil

1 tablespoon minced fresh lemon balm

3 tablespoons unsalted butter

1 tablespoon olive oil

Preheat the oven to 350°F.

In a large bowl, whisk the eggs with a fork until blended. Stir in the mint, parsley, chervil, and lemon balm.

In a large, ovenproof nonstick pan over medium heat, warm the butter and olive oil. Pour in the egg-herb mixture and let the bottom set for 30 seconds, then, with a nonstick spatula, spread the top of the mixture around until most of the egg feels set but the top is still wet, 2 to 3 minutes.

Turn out the frittata onto a plate, then slide it back into the pan, cooked-side up. Finish in the oven until the bottom of the frittata is completely set, 3 to 5 minutes. Serve immediately.

POLENTA WITH WHITE PEACH, RICOTTA, AND ROSEMARY

Makes 4 servings

We talked about polenta in the Land section, but the addition of fresh sheep's milk ricotta (also known as "basket ricotta" because it's hung to dry and drain in little baskets), which you can find easily in northern FVG, makes this dish very mountainous indeed. This recipe is all about simplicity and the essence of flavor: long, slow cooking of the polenta grain; a fresh and juicy summer peach; and not-your-average-soft-supermarket ricotta. We often think of the Carnic Mountains as colder-climate due to their elevation, but the summer months bring heat and dryness and lighter fare. Lachlan especially likes to take dishes and products that are thought to be rich and brighten them up. This is polenta at its most refreshing.

Note

Your local cheesemonger or Whole Foods will have basket ricotta.

3 quarts water

1½ teaspoons fine sea salt

1½ cups rustic polenta integrale or coarse-grind polenta (see page 72)

2 ripe white peaches

6 ounces sheep's milk basket ricotta, sliced into 4 pieces

Leaves from 1 rosemary sprig, minced

2 tablespoons extra-virgin olive oil

In a Dutch oven over high heat, combine the water and salt and bring to a boil. Slowly pour in the polenta, letting it run in thin streams through your fingers while whisking constantly to avoid any clumping. Bring the mixture to a boil, still whisking nonstop. Once the polenta starts to bubble and thicken slightly, after about 5 minutes, turn the heat to low and cover. Simmer for 1½ hours, whisking every 10 minutes or so, making sure to scrape the bottom and sides of the pot, until the polenta is fully cooked. The polenta should be extremely tender and soft.

Spoon ¾ cup polenta into each shallow bowl. Peel and slice the peaches and arrange in each bowl. Lay a slice of ricotta alongside each portion of peach. Sprinkle with the rosemary and drizzle with the olive oil. Serve immediately.

CHILLED TOMATO AND PEACH SOUP

Makes 4 servings; about 1 quart

I am a huge fan of chilled soups in the summer months. I typically like to use tomatoes or stone fruits as a base. On a trip to the Carnic Alps one summer, we came across the most beautiful large tomatoes and baby white peaches. They became the basis for this recipe. The secret touch is fresh lovage. I absolutely love its celery character; it adds the perfect perfume to this refreshing summer soup.

YOU WILL NEED
Immersion blender (optional)

1 ripe peach, peeled, pitted, and diced

½ English cucumber, peeled and diced

8 cherry tomatoes, halved, or 2 large heirloom tomatoes, diced

Leaves from 2 lovage sprigs

Leaves from 2 basil sprigs

1 tablespoon fine sea salt

1 teaspoon freshly ground black pepper

1 tablespoon extra-virgin olive oil, plus more for drizzling

4 tablespoons fresh ricotta

In a blender or using an immersion blender, combine the peach, cucumber, tomatoes, lovage, basil (reserving 4 leaves for garnish), salt, pepper, and the olive oil. Blend until smooth, then refrigerate until nicely chilled, about 30 minutes.

Ladle the soup into bowls and garnish each with a generous drizzle of olive oil, 1 tablespoon fresh ricotta, and a reserved basil leaf. Serve immediately.

ZUPPA DI AGLIO

(Garlic Soup)

Makes 4 to 6 servings; about 1½ quarts

Bear's garlic, aka *aglio orsino*, aka ramps, can be found in the Carnic and Julian Alps, both in the wild and at any local supermarket. Beyond having medicinal properties for indigestion and rashes (helpful when traveling in the mountains), it's also intensely flavorful. At Frasca, we have served garlic soup many different ways, but this one in particular, with cured garlic bulbs, makes for a great meal opener, especially in the wintertime when accompanied by a glass of Ribolla Gialla. The flavor of the soup is potent but delicious. If ramps are in season, you can substitute a pound of ramps for the garlic in this recipe.

¼ cup olive oil

10 garlic cloves, minced

3 cups peeled and sliced russet potatoes

1 quart vegetable stock or chicken stock or low-sodium broth, plus more as needed

Fine sea salt

Extra-virgin olive oil for drizzling

1 to 1½ cups bread croutons

In a Dutch oven or heavy pot over medium-low heat, warm the olive oil. Add the minced garlic, stir, and gently sauté, making sure not to let it color, until the garlic aroma starts to be released, about 1 minute. Stir in the potato slices, turn the heat to low, cover, and sweat until the potatoes start to break down, 7 to 8 minutes—stir every 2 minutes or so to make sure the garlic doesn't burn.

Pour the vegetable stock into the pot, increase the heat to high, and bring to a boil. Turn the heat to low, cover, and simmer until the potatoes are tender, about 25 minutes. Transfer to a blender and blend until smooth, thinning out with water or additional stock as needed. Season with salt.

Ladle the soup into bowls, drizzle with extra-virgin olive oil, and top with the croutons. Serve immediately.

PORCINI SOUP

Makes 4 to 6 servings; about 2 quarts

Of all the mushrooms in Friuli, porcini—which are known for their depth of flavor and meaty texture—are the most famous. The key to this simple soup is a great mushroom broth. Without it, the soup lacks the real mushroom flavor needed to make it as delicious as it can be. The soup should be served piping hot so it can gently cook all the raw mushrooms you shave into it just before serving.

YOU WILL NEED
Mandoline

1 cup dry orzo pasta

1 tablespoon olive oil

2 large russet potatoes

3 porcini mushrooms,
or 3 cups button mushrooms

6 cups Mushroom Stock
(page 210)

1 tablespoon kosher salt

Pinch of freshly ground
black pepper

6 flat-leaf parsley sprigs,
coarsely chopped

1 rosemary sprig, minced

Bring a large saucepan of salted water to a boil. Add the orzo and cook until tender, 8 to 10 minutes. Drain, stir in the olive oil (so the pasta doesn't stick), and set aside.

Bring a second saucepan of salted water to a boil. Add the potatoes and cook until fork-tender, about 30 minutes. When cool enough to handle, peel the potatoes and cut into ½-inch cubes. Set aside.

Using a mandoline or very sharp knife, slice the mushrooms about ¹⁄₁₆ inch thick and set aside.

In a large saucepan over medium-high heat, warm the mushroom stock until simmering and then season with the salt and pepper. Stir in the potatoes and cooked orzo.

Ladle the soup into bowls. Garnish with the parsley, rosemary, and shaved fresh mushrooms. Serve immediately.

Mushroom Stock
Makes about 3 quarts

We use this stock to make our porcini soup and risotto. As a result, we purchase *a lot* of fresh porcini mushrooms each autumn when they are in season and make a ton of stock (100 to 120 gallons), which we then freeze to use throughout the year. If you are imagining cauldrons and stockpots bubbling over with a pungent fungi fragrance permeating the air, you have it right.

This is definitely the time and place to use more beaten-up or less-pretty porcinis. If you missed the narrow window in September to October when porcini can be found, you can definitely make a rich stock using a mixture of other mushrooms, such as button, cremini, or shiitake. You may also discover that your greengrocer keeps frozen porcini "in the back" to offer to clients year-round; just ask! I like to keep this stock's ingredients to a minimum—adding vegetables could sweeten it or detract from the overall mushroom flavor.

Note
If procuring this amount of porcini is difficult, you can use a mixture of fresh mushrooms and dried porcini to make the stock, such as 5 cups button mushrooms and 1 cup dried porcini.

¼ cup grapeseed oil

6 cups sliced fresh porcini mushrooms

3 shallots, minced

1½ cups dry white wine

3 rosemary sprigs

3 quarts water

In a large Dutch oven or heavy pot over medium-high heat, warm the grapeseed oil. Add the mushrooms and shallots and sauté, stirring occasionally, allowing them to caramelize, about 15 minutes. Once the mushrooms have a nice golden brown color and have released much of their water, add the wine and rosemary and deglaze the pan, scraping up any browned bits with a wooden spoon.

Turn the heat to high and cook until most of the wine has been absorbed or is evaporated, about 5 minutes. Pour in the water and bring to a boil. Turn the heat to low and simmer for 1 hour.

Strain the stock through a fine-mesh sieve and transfer to two 1½-quart airtight containers. Store in the refrigerator for up to 1 week or in the freezer for up to 2 months.

BREAD SOUP WITH GUANCIALE

Makes 4 servings

Sometimes referred to as *panada*, this typical Italian bread soup is made Friulian with the addition of Montasio and guanciale (cured pork jowl). It is a staple for the people of Ovaro, a high-altitude village that can be cut off from bigger towns (and fresh supplies) for weeks on end during winter. This soup is made from whatever pantry items are available during the snowy months.

Note

We buy our guanciale online from 'Nduja Artisans Salumeria, but your local charcuterie maker likely sells guanciale too.

¼ cup unsalted butter

⅔ cup finely diced yellow onion

Fine sea salt

4 cups cubed country bread, crusts removed

3 cups chicken stock or low-sodium chicken broth

1 cup grated Montasio cheese

¼ pound guanciale, diced into ¼-inch cubes

2 large garlic cloves, minced

In a Dutch oven over medium-low heat, melt the butter. Add the onion and a pinch of salt, stir, cover, and sweat until translucent, 5 to 7 minutes. Add the bread cubes and mix thoroughly with the onion. Pour in the chicken stock, increase the heat to medium-high, and simmer until the bread has fully absorbed the stock and starts to break down, 15 to 20 minutes. Add the Montasio and stir until melted, about 3 minutes. Keep the soup warm.

In small frying pan over medium heat, cook the guanciale and render until crispy, about 5 minutes. Add the garlic and cook until lightly browned, about 3 minutes more. Remove from the heat.

Ladle the soup into shallow bowls and top with the guanciale mixture. Serve immediately.

MONTASIO AND PROSCIUTTO BRODO WITH NETTLE AND SPINACH CANEDERLI

Makes 4 servings; about 20 golf ball–size dumplings

Whoever came up with the first *canederli* (dumplings) was a home-economics master. With origins in South Tyrol, these dumplings testify to the thrift and adaptation of mountain living. Canederlis can be made from anything, really; you essentially knead together whatever remaining ingredients are in the pantry. In this case, our pantry is full of stale bread, nettles, and spinach, formed together to create the substance of the dish. The flavor comes from the brodo that is made of chicken stock, cheese rinds, and prosciutto or speck. Seeing as we're in the mountains, we've gone top-shelf and used local Wolf prosciutto, which brings a nice salt content (as a result, lean toward the low-sodium side for the stock). Macerated wine, be it Radikon or Gravner, sings with this dish.

Notes

A specialty Italian grocer will have Parmigiano rinds and prosciutto ends to sell at a discount. If you don't see them in one of the cheese or salumi fridges, you may have to ask.

Don't forget to wear gloves when handling fresh stinging nettles, which can be foraged or found in the spring and summer at farmers' markets.

BRODO

4 cups chicken stock or low-sodium chicken broth	¼ pound Montasio or Parmigiano-Reggiano cheese rinds
¼ pound prosciutto ends or trimmings, cubed	

CANEDERLI

3 cups diced stale white bread (crusts removed)	1 cup packed young nettle leaves
2 cups milk, warmed	3 eggs, beaten
1 cup packed baby spinach leaves	Finely grated zest of 1 lemon
	Fine sea salt and freshly ground black pepper

Fine sea salt and freshly ground black pepper

To make the brodo: In a Dutch oven over medium-high heat, combine the chicken stock, prosciutto ends, and cheese rinds and bring to a simmer. Turn the heat to low and simmer for 45 minutes.

To make the canederli: While the brodo is simmering, soak the bread cubes in the warm milk for 30 minutes.

Meanwhile, bring a pot of salted water to a boil. Add the spinach and nettle leaves and blanch for 30 seconds to wilt. Drain, squeeze out the excess liquid, and finely chop the leaves.

Squeeze the excess milk from the soaked bread cubes. In a large bowl, combine the bread with the spinach, nettles, eggs, and lemon zest. Mix well with your hands until homogenous; the dough should come together but feel slightly tacky, then season with salt and pepper.

Moisten your hands (keep a small bowl of water nearby) and manually shape the bread mixture into small balls, each about the size of a golf ball. You can also use a small ice-cream scoop to portion the canederli equally, then roll them by hand. Set aside on a plate.

Strain the brodo and discard the cheese rinds and prosciutto trimmings. Season with salt and pepper and return to the pot over medium-low heat. Slide the canederli into the warm brodo and simmer until the dumplings are heated through, 8 to 12 minutes. Remove the canederli with a slotted spoon and transfer to shallow serving bowls, then ladle in 1 cup of brodo per bowl. Serve immediately.

SPAGHETTI CON FUNGHI AL CARTOCCIO

(Baked Spaghetti with Mushrooms in Parchment)

Makes 4 to 6 servings

Imagine a dish that arrives in a little parchment-wrapped package (known as a *cartoccio*, or cartouche) like a baked gift from the spaghetti gods. You open it up, and with the warm steam comes the scent of olive oil, parsley, white wine, and wild mushrooms. Bam! That's this dish right here. It's very simple to make and is also a great way to get children to eat fungi.

YOU WILL NEED
Four to six 15-inch parchment-paper squares

1 pound dry spaghetti	Fine sea salt
¼ cup olive oil	½ cup dry white wine
2 tablespoons unsalted butter	1 cup vegetable stock
1 pound mixed fresh wild mushrooms, such as black trumpets or chanterelles, trimmed	¼ cup minced fresh flat-leaf parsley
	2 tablespoons extra-virgin olive oil
2 small shallots, minced	

Preheat the oven to 400°F.

Bring a large pot of salted water to a boil. Add the spaghetti and cook for 2 minutes short of the timing for al dente on the package.

While the pasta is cooking, in a large sauté pan over high heat, warm the olive oil and butter. Add the mushrooms and sauté until wilted, about 5 minutes. Push the mushrooms to the side of the pan, turn the heat to medium, add the shallots, and sauté until translucent, about 3 minutes, seasoning with salt as you go. Stir the mushrooms into the shallots, add the wine, and cook until it is almost completely absorbed, about 3 minutes. Pour in the vegetable stock, turn the heat to high, bring to a boil, then turn the heat to low and simmer until the cooking juices reduce slightly, about 5 minutes.

Drain the undercooked pasta and stir it into the sauce, mix in the parsley, and then stir in the extra-virgin olive oil.

On a work surface, lay out one parchment square per person. Place one portion of pasta onto the center of each square. Moisten the edges of the parchment with water and fold up into a triangle shape, crimping all along the edges to make a seal. Gently lift and transfer to a baking sheet. Repeat with the remaining squares.

Bake until the parchments puff up (from the steam inside), about 5 minutes. Use a large flat spatula to transfer each parcel to a plate.

Serve immediately, letting your dinner guests open their own cartoccio!

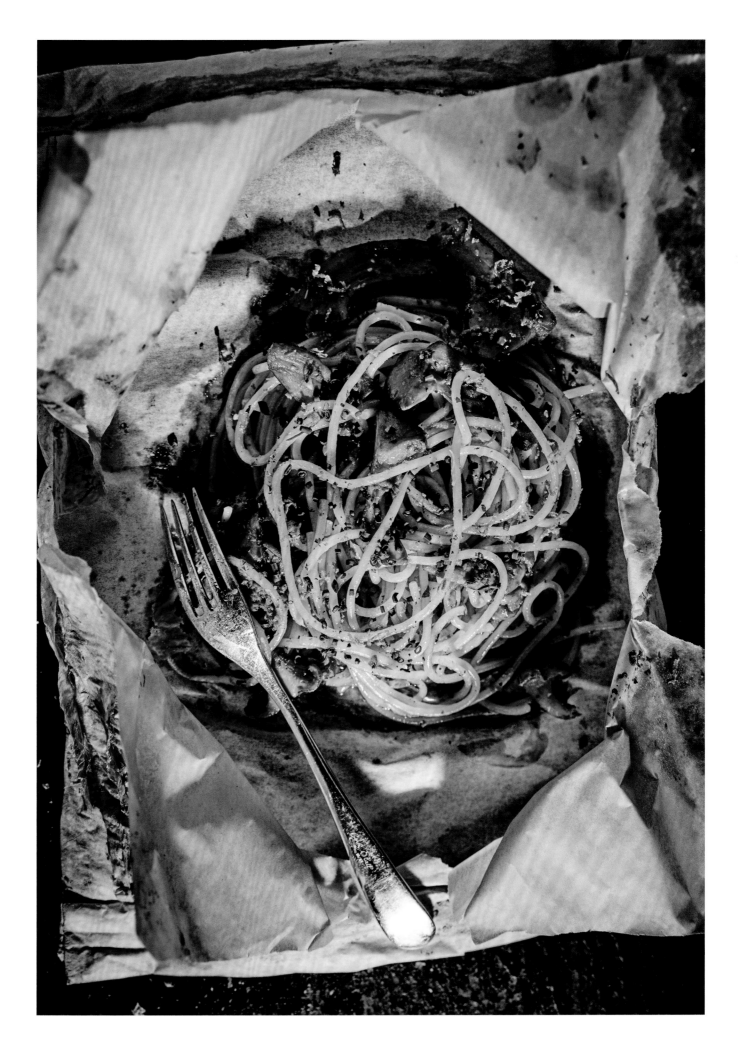

GIRINI DI PASTA

(Spelt Pasta "Tadpoles" with Zucchini and Rosemary)

Makes 4 servings

This squiggly, spaetzle-like pasta (*girini* means "tadpoles" in Italian) is fun to make. You pass an egg-flour batter through a potato ricer to make small "crumbs" of pasta, which are boiled and then combined with seasonal greens and other ingredients such as San Daniele ham and cheese. Spaetzle is found throughout Germany and Austria, and this tradition of boiled dough has made its way to Friuli via the adjoining Alto Adige/South Tyrol region. Much like forming gnocchi and spaetzle, girini require a lightness and consistency of touch that only come from making them often. It'll take you some time to perfect the visuals of this recipe; in the meantime, keep trying and have a glass of Doro Princic Pinot Bianco while you do. This dish is especially tasty when topped with grated Montasio.

Note
Spelt flour can be found at good grocers, or order online.

YOU WILL NEED
Potato ricer or a colander with large holes

⅔ cup spelt flour

⅓ cup all-purpose flour

1 teaspoon fine sea salt

2 eggs

¼ cup water, plus more as needed

2 tablespoons extra-virgin olive oil, plus more for drizzling

Two ⅛-inch-thick slices guanciale, cut into ½-inch squares

½ zucchini, coarsely grated

½ teaspoon minced fresh rosemary

2 tablespoons finely grated Montasio cheese

½ lemon

In a medium bowl, whisk together both flours, the salt, eggs, and water to make a smooth but thick, spoonable batter, adding a splash more water as needed. Refrigerate until chilled, about 1 hour.

Bring a large pot of salted water to a simmer over high heat.

Spoon one-fourth of the batter into a potato ricer, using a second spoon to scrape the batter off the first spoon. Hold the potato ricer directly over the simmering water, then press the top handle of the ricer to squeeze the batter through, into the water. Immediately stir the noodles well with a long spatula or wooden spoon.

Once the pasta floats to the surface and tastes cooked, after about 1 minute, remove it with a slotted spoon or spider and place it into a bowl. Splash the pasta with the olive oil. Cook the remaining batter in three more batches, stirring it well in the bowl after transferring, to prevent sticking.

Line a plate with paper towels.

In a medium nonstick frying pan over medium-low heat, cook the guanciale without stirring until it has rendered most of its fat, about 3 minutes. Stir the guanciale and cook the other side until crispy, about 3 minutes more. Transfer the guanciale to the prepared plate. Drain most of the guanciale fat from the pan.

Add the zucchini and rosemary to the pan, turn the heat to medium, and stir to warm, about 30 seconds. Stir in the girini to combine and reheat.

Divide the noodles among four shallow bowls. Top each with the crispy guanciale, the Montasio, and a squeeze of fresh lemon juice. Serve immediately.

SQUASH GNOCCHI WITH SMOKED RICOTTA SAUCE

Makes 4 servings

As Bobby tells it, "I don't think there is an ingredient that can outdo the effect that smoked ricotta had on Lachlan, Danette, Nate Ready, and me when we first tried it in the Carnic Alps. It's not just the flavor, it's not just the aromatics; it's the whole intense, heady experience that you will never forget. It's something that will always remind us of the Alps in Friuli. To this day, we always have a dish on the menu using smoked ricotta, and when I take that plate to a table, I get a smile on my face like I did when I first smelled this ingredient."

Note

We love to use heirloom red kuri squash in this recipe for its unique flavor. Because the availability and water content of heirloom squashes can vary, this recipe calls for butternut squash. Feel free to experiment with heirloom squash after you've made this recipe with butternut squash—you will likely need to use much less flour because red kuri and other heirlooms can contain less water (the more flour you use, the less tender the gnocchi).

YOU WILL NEED
Potato ricer or food mill
Bench scraper
Gnocchi board

SQUASH GNOCCHI

One 2-pound butternut squash	1 egg yolk
Extra-virgin olive oil for brushing, plus 1 tablespoon	1 tablespoon whole-milk ricotta
Fine sea salt	1 tablespoon mascarpone
1 cup all-purpose flour, plus more as needed	

SMOKED RICOTTA SAUCE

2 cups coarsely grated Indoor Smoked Ricotta (recipe follows)	1 cup heavy cream, plus more as needed

To make the gnocchi: Preheat the oven to 325°F. Line a baking sheet with parchment paper and lightly flour a second baking sheet.

Cut the squash in half; scrape out and discard the seeds. Brush the cut sides of the squash with olive oil and season with salt. Place the squash cut-side down on the parchment-lined baking sheet. Cover with aluminum foil, wrap tightly, and bake until fork-tender, about 45 minutes.

Scoop the squash flesh into a bowl and pass it through a potato ricer or food mill directly onto a clean working surface. Using a bench scraper, spread out the squash to cool slightly.

Sift the flour onto the squash, then drop the egg yolk, whole-milk ricotta, mascarpone, and 1 tablespoon olive oil over the squash. Use the bench scraper to pick up the squash and fold it and the other ingredients into each other. Repeat several times until combined. Use your hands to gather the dough up into a ball. The mixture should feel moist and tacky but hold together enough to roll out; you can add more flour, 1 tablespoon at a time, as needed, but be careful not to add too much flour or over-knead as this will result in much less tender gnocchi. Let the dough rest for 30 minutes (this will also help the mixture set a little).

Using the bench scraper, cut the dough into six pieces and roll each into a ½-inch-thick log.

Next, cut each log into ½-inch pieces. Using your thumb, roll and press each piece along a lightly floured gnocchi board to create the distinctive ridges and curled shape of gnocchi, then transfer to the flour-dusted baking sheet. (If not cooking immediately, the gnocchi can be frozen on the baking sheet, then transferred to a resealable plastic bag and kept in the freezer for up to 1 month. Do not thaw before cooking.)

Bring a large pot of salted water to a boil.

To make the sauce: While the water is coming to a boil, in a nonstick frying pan over medium heat, toast the smoked ricotta until nicely browned, about 8 minutes, stirring every 2 minutes or so. Pour in the cream and turn the heat to low. Stir the ricotta and cream together and cook until slightly thickened, about 2 minutes. Remove from the heat, pour into a blender, and blend until smooth, adding a splash more cream if needed to loosen the sauce. Return the sauce to the pan and keep warm over very low heat.

Working in two batches, cook the gnocchi in the boiling water until they float to the surface, then simmer for 1 to 2 minutes more until tender and cooked through, 3 to 4 minutes total. Using a slotted spoon, transfer the gnocchi to the simmering sauce.

Spoon the gnocchi and sauce into individual shallow bowls. Serve immediately.

Indoor Smoked Ricotta
Makes ½ pound

This is a fail-proof way to add a singular smoked flavor to ricotta without having to wash all of your clothing.

YOU WILL NEED
Old roasting pan or cast-iron pan
Handful of wood chips
Small wire rack

½ pound ricotta salata

Cover the bottom of an old roasting pan or cast-iron pan with aluminum foil. Put a handful of wood chips on the foil. Next, set a small rack inside the pan and on top of the wood chips.

Put the ricotta in a small heatproof bowl and have more foil ready next to the stove, as well as a container of water to stop the smoking process at the end.

Place the pan over high heat. The wood chips will self-ignite and start to smoke within 10 minutes. When the smoking starts to happen, place the bowl of ricotta on the rack and cover the pan tightly with foil. Turn on the hood fan and open a window to keep your kitchen from smoking out. Turn the heat to medium and smoke for 5 minutes, then turn off the heat and keep smoking the ricotta until the smoke has fully infused the cheese, about 10 minutes more. Discard the foil, remove the bowl, and extinguish the wood chips with the water. The ricotta will keep in an airtight container, in the refrigerator, for up to 1 week.

MRS. B'S CANDIED FRUIT AND RICOTTA CJALSÒNS

Makes 6 servings; about 40 dumplings

Perhaps the most quintessential pasta dish in the Carnic Alps, these candied fruit and ricotta dumplings are rumored to have ties to the *Cramârs*, nomadic salesmen from Carnia who traveled through the mountains of Austria-Hungary in the Middle Ages and beyond with wooden cabinets strapped to their backs, offering spices, fabrics, and miscellaneous wares. Legend has it that when they returned home, their wives would make these little dumplings, or pasta pockets, filling them with candied fruit and unsold spices.

While staying at the base of Monte Zoncolan, we met the Brovedan family, our neighbors for a week. We mentioned our love of cjalsòns ("jahls-owns") and that we'd heard the best in the region were made in the next town over. In typical Friulian fashion, we were corrected: Mrs. B, Erika's mother, makes the best. The next day, the entire Brovedan family came over to our rental apartment to give us a tutorial. The beauty of this dish is that you can give it your own twist by adjusting the spice ratios and fruit content.

You know that weird time between Christmas and New Year's Day, when you're unsure what day it is *and* you have fresh nutmeg, cinnamon, and leftover candied fruits in your pantry? This would be *the* recipe for using up those misfit ingredients.

Notes

Ideally, the filling should be refrigerated for 6 hours, or overnight, allowing the flavors to really come together. The cjalsòns dough can also be made a day ahead. Plan accordingly.

This dough includes a fair amount of milk, which makes it more supple and easier to work with than a typical pasta dough. Once cooked, the dough takes on a milky white, almost translucent, color.

YOU WILL NEED

Pasta machine or stand mixer fitted with pasta attachment
3-inch cookie cutter
Piping bag fitted with medium plain tip (optional)

FILLING

1 cup fresh ricotta, drained	¾ cup grated smoked ricotta salata (see page 219)
1 tablespoon finely chopped candied orange	2½ tablespoons sugar
2 teaspoons finely chopped candied cherry	¼ teaspoon kosher salt
2 teaspoons finely chopped dried papaya	1 teaspoon dark or light rum
2 teaspoons finely chopped dried apricot	1 teaspoon cocoa powder
	⅛ teaspoon ground cinnamon
1 tablespoon raisins, soaked in warm water for 30 minutes and then drained	½ cup cherry jam
	2 cups shortbread or biscotti crumbs

CJALSÒNS DOUGH

3 cups 00 flour (see Note, page 88) or all-purpose flour, plus more as needed	¾ cup whole milk
	¼ cup water, plus more as needed
1 tablespoon kosher salt	Semolina flour for dusting

¼ cup unsalted butter, melted	⅓ cup grated smoked ricotta salata (see page 219)
1 teaspoon cocoa powder	

continued

To make the filling: In a large bowl, combine the fresh ricotta, candied orange, candied cherry, dried papaya, dried apricot, raisins, and ricotta salata, using a wooden spoon or spatula to mix. Stir in the sugar, salt, rum, cocoa powder, cinnamon, cherry jam, and shortbread crumbs. Mix well, but be careful not to overdo it and render the filling mushy. Cover and refrigerate for at least 4 hours or up to 6 hours.

To make the dough: Put the flour and salt in a large bowl, make a well at the center, and add the milk and water to the well. Using a wooden spoon, stir to combine until a dough begins to come together, then shape the dough into a ball. If the dough feels sticky, add more flour; if the dough will not form into a ball, add a splash more water.

Lightly dust a counter with all-purpose flour. Turn out the dough and knead until it feels elastic and looks smooth. Wrap the dough tightly in plastic and refrigerate for at least 30 minutes, or up to overnight, to rest and hydrate.

Heavily dust a baking sheet with semolina flour. Slice the dough ½ inch thick. Keep the dough covered while working with one slice at a time. Flatten the slice a little with the palm of your hand. Roll the dough through the widest setting of a pasta machine (or attachment, if you're using a stand mixer), dusting with flour along the way to ensure the dough doesn't stick, but not too much as you don't want the dough to become dry. Fold the sheet of dough in half onto itself and roll it through this initial setting five to ten times, folding it again after each pass.

Change the machine setting to the next, more-narrow setting, and roll the sheet through once. Continue with the next more-narrow setting. You'll notice your sheet will become longer and longer as you work it through each successive setting. Keep rolling until Setting 7 (on most pasta machines) or thin enough that you can almost see your hand through the dough. Lay the pasta sheet out on the prepared baking sheet. Repeat the rolling procedure with the remaining slices of dough.

Dust a work surface with semolina flour and spread out the sheets of rolled dough. Use a 3-inch cookie cutter to cut out as many circles of dough as you can, gathering and rerolling the scraps as needed—you should have about forty circles of dough.

Set up an assembly line with the dough circles, filling, a small bowl of water, and a semolina-dusted baking sheet. Using a teaspoon (or a piping bag fitted with a medium plain tip), place 2 teaspoons of filling in the center of each dough circle. Wet the edge of the circles, then fold the dough over the filling to form half-moons, pressing on the outside edges with your fingers to seal completely. (To shape the cjalsòns like Mrs. B, use your thumb and index finger to laterally crimp the sealed edge of the half-moon as you would a pie crust.) Transfer to the prepared baking sheet.

Bring a large pot of unsalted water to a boil. Add all the stuffed pasta and cook until the pasta is tender and the filling is heated through, 3 to 4 minutes after the water returns to a consistent simmer; then, using a slotted spoon or skimmer, gently transfer the cjalsòns to a large bowl.

Drizzle the dumplings with the melted butter and, using a fine-mesh sieve, dust with the cocoa powder, then sprinkle with the ricotta salata. Serve immediately.

POTATO AND HERB CJALSÒNS

Makes 6 servings; about 40 dumplings

Before we met Mrs. B and were bowled over by her sweet cjalsòns (see page 221), we had tried savory cjalsòns all over Friuli's mountainous region. It's fair to say that we tasted far and wide for the best version of this savory pasta classic. One summer day, while having lunch at Osteria da Alvise in the tiny mountain village of Sutrio, some fifteen kilometers away from Mrs. B's village, we came across these savory beauties. Lore has it that cjalsòns were actually first made in Sutrio, so it's perhaps not surprising that these dumplings were so out of this world. The key to this dish is two-fold: really great herbs and a dough that's been rolled out until very thin. I have had this same filling inside a typical egg-noodle dough (see page 89), and while the texture of the dough felt familiar, it lacked the transportive authenticity that this very specific milk-and-flour dough gives the dumpling. The herbs in the filling really shine through when cooked because the dough doesn't overpower the delicate flavors.

YOU WILL NEED
Potato ricer
3-inch cookie cutter
Piping bag fitted with medium plain tip (optional)

2 large Yukon gold potatoes (see Note, page 91)

1 tablespoon unsalted butter, plus ¼ cup melted

1 cup minced yellow onion

2 tablespoons golden raisins, soaked in warm water to cover for 30 minutes

1 teaspoon minced fresh mint leaves

1 teaspoon minced fresh flat-leaf parsley

1 teaspoon minced fresh lovage or celery leaves

Fine sea salt

Semolina flour for dusting

1 recipe Cjalsòns Dough (see page 221), chilled, rested, and cut into forty 3-inch circles

¼ cup grated ricotta salata

Bring a large saucepan of salted water to a boil over high heat. Add the potatoes and cook until tender, about 30 minutes.

While the potatoes are cooking, in a medium sauté pan over medium-low heat, melt the 1 tablespoon butter. Add the onion and gently sauté until translucent, about 8 minutes. Stir in the raisins.

Pass the hot potatoes, skin-on, through a ricer into a large bowl. Add the onion and raisins and the minced herbs and stir with a spatula to combine. Season with salt and set aside.

Dust a baking sheet with semolina. Set up an assembly line with the dough circles, potato mixture, a small bowl of water, and the prepared baking sheet. Using a teaspoon (or a piping bag fitted with a medium plain tip), place 1 teaspoon of filling in the center of each dough circle. Wet the edge of the circles, then fold the dough over the filling to form half-moons, pressing on the outside edges with your fingers to seal completely. Use your thumb and index finger to laterally crimp the sealed edge of the half-moon as you would a pie crust. Transfer to the prepared baking sheet.

Bring a large pot of salted water to a rolling boil. Add all the stuffed pasta and cook until the pasta is tender and the filling is heated through, 3 to 4 minutes after the water returns to a consistent simmer; then, using a slotted spoon or skimmer, gently transfer the cjalsòns to a large bowl or place five or six dumplings in individual bowls.

Drizzle the dumplings with the melted butter and sprinkle with the ricotta salata. Serve immediately.

MUSHROOM RISOTTO

Makes 4 servings

We could have included an entire section of risottos in this book: *riso marinara, riso con tartufo nero, riso con funghi. . . .* Over the years, we've learned a lot when it comes to making risotto—cook it slowly, cook it in a flavorful broth, let the rice rest toward the end of cooking so it can absorb even more of the broth's flavors, and, most important, only cook the rice until it's *al dente*! Too many risottos in this world are overcooked and mushy, lacking the elegance of a well-prepared dish. Be prepared to stir the rice almost continuously. This is a meditative dish that demands your vigilance, but it comes together in less than 20 minutes.

This risotto is inspired by some fresh porcini we found while cycling up Monte Crostis. A fairly treacherous route tucked into the steep hillside outside the village of Comeglians, the climb is most known for its tricky descent and, famously, for being removed at the last minute from the 2011 Giro d'Italia course (it was too narrow for the support cars!).

Notes

There are many different types of risotto grains to choose from, but at Frasca, we prefer to use either Carnaroli or Vialone Nano rice. The general rule of thumb is, if you want the risotto to soak up the broth flavor and you don't plan to add cheese or butter to finish, Vialone Nano is your best bet because it soaks up twice its weight in liquid. For other risottos, we always use Carnaroli.

If you're making this dish when fresh (or frozen) porcini are not available, substitute other mushrooms of your choosing.

¾ cup extra-virgin olive oil

½ cup finely diced yellow onion

1 garlic clove, smashed and peeled

1 large fresh sage leaf

1 rosemary sprig, plus 1 teaspoon minced fresh rosemary leaves

Fine sea salt

1½ quarts Mushroom Stock (page 210)

¾ cup Vialone Nano rice (see Note)

½ cup dry white wine

2 cups thinly sliced fresh porcini mushrooms

1 tablespoon freshly squeezed lemon juice, or to taste

Freshly ground black pepper

In a wide heavy pot over medium-low heat, warm ½ cup of the olive oil. Add the onion, garlic, sage, rosemary sprig, and ½ teaspoon salt and stir to coat. Cook, stirring often, until the onion starts to soften and become translucent, taking care not to burn it, about 5 minutes.

In a saucepan over medium heat, warm the mushroom stock to a simmer, then keep hot over low heat.

Add the rice to the onion and stir until nicely coated. Turn the heat to medium and cook until toasted—it will start to smell nutty—30 to 45 seconds. Pour in the wine and, stirring continuously, cook until the wine has almost completely evaporated, 30 to 45 seconds. Stir in the porcini, followed by ½ cup hot mushroom stock, and keep stirring until the rice has absorbed almost all of the stock.

Turn the heat to medium-low. Continue to add stock to the rice, ¼ cup at a time, stirring continuously and repeating each addition of stock as the rice absorbs the liquid fully. The more you stir, the creamier your risotto will be. After 13 minutes—this is our *al dente* moment—stir in a final ¼ cup stock, turn off the heat, and let the risotto rest for 5 minutes. Discard the rosemary sprig.

Return the risotto to low heat and slowly drizzle in the remaining ¼ cup olive oil, stirring nonstop. The risotto will become creamier as the broth and oil emulsify nicely.

Finally, stir in the lemon juice and minced rosemary, adjusting the consistency of the risotto with any remaining mushroom stock as needed. The consistency should be thick but somewhat soupy. Season with salt and pepper and additional lemon juice, if necessary. Serve immediately.

Ovaro, Carnic Alps

BEEF SHORT RIBS WITH HORSERADISH AND APPLE

Makes 4 to 6 servings

Horseradish and apple is a combination you find often in Friuli, especially in the Carnic Mountains. Here, we stew the apples and pickle the horseradish to serve alongside braised beef. In the Frasca kitchen, we practice cooking the same thing two different ways. In this particular case, we love the texture of a perfectly braised piece of meat—it's so tender, it just falls apart with the push of a fork. But to take it to the next level, we finish the braised meat on the grill to add a crispy exterior.

Bobby would want you to enjoy this with a glass of Le Monde Refosco from the Friuli Grave region. The wine is very bright, and perfect for this dish.

Note

Check the size of your Dutch oven versus the size of the ribs—you may need to cut the meat into pieces so the ribs can fit comfortably in the pot when you sear them.

SHORT RIBS

¼ cup olive oil	2 medium carrots, cut into ½-inch dice
3 pounds bone-in beef short ribs	4 garlic cloves, minced
Fine sea salt and freshly ground black pepper	½ cup tomato paste
1 large yellow onion, cut into ½-inch dice	2 cups red wine
	1 dried bay leaf
2 celery ribs, cut into ½-inch dice	2 thyme sprigs
	4 to 6 cups chicken stock or low-sodium chicken broth

STEWED APPLES

4 Granny Smith apples, peeled, cored, and cut into 6 wedges each	2 cups apple cider

PICKLED HORSERADISH

¼ cup grated horseradish	1 teaspoon fine sea salt
¼ cup distilled white vinegar	2 tablespoons water
1 tablespoon sugar	

To prepare the short ribs: In a large Dutch oven over medium heat, warm the olive oil. Season the short ribs with salt and pepper. Add to the Dutch oven and sear on all sides until nicely browned and caramelized, 8 to 10 minutes. Make sure not to overcrowd pot; work in two batches if necessary. Once browned, transfer the short ribs to a plate. Add the onion, celery, and carrots to the Dutch oven and brown the vegetables until caramelized, about 10 minutes. Add the garlic and sauté until aromatic, about 2 minutes. Stir in the tomato paste to coat the vegetables and toast for 1 minute. Add the red wine and deglaze the pan, scraping up any browned bits with a wooden spoon, until reduced to a thick liquid, about 5 minutes. Add the bay leaf and thyme.

Return the short ribs to the pot, cover with chicken stock (the amount will depend on how large your pot is), and bring to a boil. Then, turn the heat to medium-low, cover, and simmer gently until the meat is tender and almost falling off the bone, 2 to 2½ hours. Transfer the meat to a plate.

Preheat a gas grill with burners on high, or preheat the broiler in your oven.

Skim off and discard any excess fat from the braising liquid. Turn the heat to medium and reduce the liquid until it reaches sauce consistency, about 15 minutes. Season with salt and pepper. Keep warm.

To stew the apples: In a saucepan over medium-low heat, combine the apple wedges and apple cider and poach, uncovered, until tender and the liquid is reduced by half, about 10 minutes. Keep warm.

To make the pickled horseradish: Put the grated horseradish in a heatproof bowl or jar. In a small saucepan, combine the vinegar, sugar, salt, and water and bring to a boil. Stir immediately to dissolve the salt and sugar, then pour the hot liquid over the horseradish. Set aside to cool.

Lay the meat on the grill and cook until nicely charred on both sides, 7 to 8 minutes total. Transfer the meat to a large shallow bowl and spoon over the reduced sauce. Serve with the stewed apples and the pickled horseradish on the side.

BEEF RAGÙ WITH SOFT CREAMY POLENTA

Makes 6 servings

One cold morning in Ovaro, a little village just ten kilometers from the base of Monte Zoncolan, we unwrapped a thinly sliced beef shoulder that we had purchased from our local butcher and with which we were planning to make a simple ragù for dinner. We got the meat braising before heading out on a bike ride up the mountain (one of the most demanding climbs in professional bike racing, and often part of the Giro d'Italia), so we could look forward to melt-in-your-mouth meat after those hours on the bike. To transform this ragù into a quintessential Carnic dish, we stopped by a cheese shop on our way back for some fragrant smoked ricotta to grate over the top.

Notes

Cutting the beef into small cubes shortens the cooking time; more and smaller pieces of beef in the broth also mean better flavor distribution!

You can find ricotta salata at most fine cheese shops. Pecorino Romano or even mizithra—because of its texture (it can be grated) and salinity—are two decent substitutes.

In a heavy pot over high heat, warm the olive oil until shimmering but not smoking. Add the beef and let it brown nicely, 1 to 2 minutes on each side. Stir in the onion, carrots, and celery and cook until they are browned, 4 to 6 minutes. Add the tomato paste and stir to combine, cooking the paste for 1 to 2 minutes until well combined. Stir in the salt, add the rosemary and wine, and simmer vigorously until most of the wine has evaporated, about 3 minutes. Add the beef stock, let the liquid come back up to a simmer, then turn the heat to low and cover.

Cook for 1 hour, then remove the cover and cook for another hour, until the beef is tender and the broth has reduced by about one-third into a sauce syrupy enough to coat the back of a spoon.

Place a generous ladle of polenta into each of six shallow bowls. Spoon the ragù over the top and sprinkle with the ricotta salata. Serve immediately.

¼ cup olive oil	1 rosemary sprig
2 pounds beef shoulder, cut into ¼-inch cubes (see Note)	1½ cups red wine
1 medium yellow onion, minced	3 quarts good-quality beef stock, chicken stock, or water
3 medium carrots, very finely diced	Soft Creamy Polenta (page 87) for serving
1 celery rib, very finely diced	1 cup grated smoked ricotta salata (see page 219 and Note)
½ tablespoon tomato paste	
2 tablespoons kosher salt	

FARRO PUDDING

Makes 4 to 6 servings

This is our interpretation of an Italian rice pudding using whole-grain farro, an heirloom variety of spelt wheat that is especially popular in Friuli. This can be served warm or cold—as a hearty breakfast in the mountains, or as a comforting dessert, as we serve it at Frasca, with diced apricots, toasted walnuts, and a drizzle of honey. Feel free to swap in other fruit, depending on your preference or the season.

Notes

Slow-roasted farro (the grain is roasted over fire, which intensifies its aroma beautifully) can be ordered online from Anson Mills. But you can also make this farro pudding with organic whole-grain farro (from Bob's Red Mill or Rustichella d'Abruzzo).

Fennel pollen can be tricky to find; try a specialty spice shop or a health food store, or order it online.

2 cups slow-roasted farro (see Note) or whole-grain farro

6 cups water

Kosher salt

2 tablespoons unsalted butter

2 tablespoons all-purpose flour

½ vanilla bean

2½ cups whole milk

¼ cup sugar

Juice of 1 lemon

¼ cup walnuts, toasted and chopped

2 apricots, pitted and diced

2 teaspoons fennel pollen (see Note)

2 tablespoons honey

In a large saucepan over medium-high heat, combine the farro, water, and 2 teaspoons salt and bring to a boil. Turn the heat to low and simmer, uncovered, until the farro is tender, 20 to 25 minutes. Drain the farro and set aside.

In a medium saucepan over low heat, melt the butter. Add the flour, whisking well to eliminate any lumps, and cook, whisking continuously, until the mixture begins to smell nutty and turns golden in color, about 2 minutes.

Slice the vanilla bean in half lengthwise and scrape the seeds into the mixture. Slowly whisk in the milk and sugar to ensure the mixture doesn't clump. Turn the heat to medium, bring to a simmer, and cook until the sauce thickens and any taste of raw flour has disappeared, about 5 minutes.

Stir the farro into the sauce—the consistency should look somewhat risotto-like. Adjust the seasoning with the lemon juice and salt.

Divide the pudding among shallow bowls and sprinkle each portion with the walnuts, apricots, and fennel pollen and drizzle with the honey. Serve immediately.

CHOCOLATE ALMONDS

Makes about 3½ cups

We're including this recipe for purely selfish reasons: We love them—plain and simple. Chocolate-coated nuts are a not-so-secret indulgence for many people, but Frasca pastry chef Alberto Hernandez truly makes the best ones. When we were shooting the photographs for this book, we had to ask Alberto to take them away because we couldn't stop eating them! These are great as an any-time-of-day snack, and even better served alongside an espresso at the end of a meal.

Note

Gianduja ("jee-ahn-doo-yah") chocolate is a Piedmont specialty and consists of sweet chocolate mixed with 30 percent hazelnut paste (think of a purer, sophisticated Nutella!). Chocolate companies such as Callebault and Valhrona offer it in semisolid cream or block form, but you can also use individually wrapped gianduja chocolates, typically found in purveyors of fine Italian products. You can also use any fine milk chocolate of your liking in this recipe.

YOU WILL NEED

Deep-frying thermometer or candy thermometer
Small silicone offset spatula (optional)

¾ cup sugar	1 teaspoon unsalted butter
2 tablespoons water	2 cups gianduja chocolate pieces (see Note)
2½ cups roasted almonds	
1 teaspoon kosher salt	2 cups cocoa powder

In a large heavy pot or Dutch oven over medium-low heat, combine the sugar and water and stir until the sugar dissolves completely and the resulting syrup reaches "soft crack" stage—285°F on a candy thermometer—about 3 minutes.

Using a wooden spoon or silicone spatula, stir the almonds into the sugar syrup, mixing continuously to coat completely. As you stir, the sugar will crystallize and form a white coat around the nuts. Keep stirring until all the nuts are evenly coated. The sugar coating may start to caramelize but don't

worry if it doesn't; give it another minute or two. Sprinkle in the salt and stir in the butter to coat the nuts.

Line a baking sheet with parchment paper and coat with nonstick cooking spray.

Spread out the nuts on the prepared baking sheet, making sure they are not touching each other.

In a heatproof bowl over a saucepan of simmering water (make sure the bottom of the bowl doesn't touch the water), regularly stir the chocolate until melted, about 2 minutes. Alternatively, microwave the chocolate in short 10- to 15-second bursts, stirring well after every burst, until completely melted. Check the temperature as you're melting the chocolate; it's important to temper it for a smooth, even, and crisp coating. If you are using small gianduja chocolates (rather than block chocolate for baking or regular milk chocolate), melt the chocolate until it registers a temperature of no more than 104°F. Remove the chocolate from the heat and allow to cool until it reaches 86°F—this will take 10 to 15 minutes (if using another kind of chocolate, refer to the temperature ranges specific to that chocolate on the back of the packaging). When the chocolate is tempered, you are ready to coat the nuts.

Put the cocoa powder in a large bowl. Set up a production line with the nuts, the melted chocolate, and the cocoa.

Working with one nut at a time, dip the nut into the chocolate, stir to coat, and lift out using a small offset spatula or your fingers, letting any excess chocolate drip off. Toss the dipped nut into the cocoa powder and shake the bowl to coat. Leave the nut in the cocoa powder while you continue to dip the remaining nuts in the melted chocolate followed by the cocoa powder. Move the coated nuts (still in the cocoa bowl) to a cool place (not the refrigerator) to rest for 1 hour, while the chocolate sets.

Toss the nuts in a sieve or colander to discard excess cocoa powder and transfer to an airtight container. The nuts will keep, at room temperature, for up to 2 weeks.

CHOCOLATE SALAMI

Makes two 7- to 8-inch salami

This dish was created by Frasca pastry chef Alberto Hernandez. It also happens to be one of the simplest dishes in the book. It's a great end-of-meal nibble for a large group, or it could be the surprise hero at your next party. The quality of the chocolate is very important because the salami is all chocolate—look for chocolate wafers made by Callebaut or Valhrona. Make sure your hands are clean before rolling the logs in the powdered sugar, and let the salami come to room temperature before serving.

Notes

Amaro Nonino Quintessentia is a digestive herbal liqueur made by the Nonino family (see page 57) in Friuli; they infuse their grappa with a blend of herbs, spices, and roots, including gentian, saffron, licorice, rhubarb, sweet and bitter orange, tamarind, quassia bark, chinchona bark, and galangal. You'll find the amaro in all good liquor stores.

Sicilian pistachios are smaller and sweeter than the ones that come from Iran, California, or Turkey. They are grown on the foothills of Mount Etna and are also known as Bronte pistachios. They can be purchased online.

¼ cup hazelnuts	1 egg
¼ cup shelled Sicilian pistachios	2 tablespoons Amaro Nonino
1 cup bittersweet chocolate fèves (discs or wafers)	½ cup biscotti crumbs
6 tablespoons unsalted butter, at room temperature	Finely grated zest of ½ orange
¼ cup granulated sugar	Confectioners' sugar for coating

Preheat the oven to 350°F.

Spread the hazelnuts and pistachios, taking care not to mix them together, on a baking sheet and toast until fragrant, 8 to 9 minutes. Skin the hazelnuts by putting them between two sheets of paper towel or a clean kitchen towel and rubbing vigorously. Pick out the hazelnuts from the dark flakes (it's okay if some patches of dark skin remain).

In a heatproof bowl over a saucepan of simmering water (make sure the bottom of the bowl doesn't touch the water), regularly stir the chocolate until melted, about 2 minutes. Alternatively, microwave the chocolate in short 10- to 15-second bursts, stirring well after every burst, until completely melted. Set the melted chocolate aside.

In the bowl of a stand mixer fitted the paddle attachment, on medium speed, cream the butter and granulated sugar until combined, about 2 minutes. Add the egg and continue to mix until incorporated. Then add the melted chocolate and amaro and mix well. Stop the mixer and, using a spatula, manually fold in the biscotti crumbs, orange zest, hazelnuts, and pistachios.

Lay out two large squares of plastic wrap on a work surface. Divide the chocolate mixture into two equal parts. Place one half of the chocolate mixture in the middle of each square and, using a spatula, spread into an approximation of a log shape, 4 to 5 inches long. Pick up the plastic wrap at either end and use it and your hands to tighten and smooth the log into a nice even shape—the log should be about 1½ inches in diameter and 7 to 8 inches long. Twist each end, as you would a candy wrapper, to tighten. Repeat with the second half of chocolate mixture. Transfer both logs to a small plate or tray and refrigerate for at least 2 hours or up to overnight.

Pour confectioners' sugar onto a large plate. Unwrap the chocolate logs and roll in the confectioners' sugar to mimic the white edible mold on an aged salami. Shake off any excess sugar. If you're feeling fancy, you can also tie up the salami in twine.

The salami will keep in an airtight container, at room temperature, for up to 1 week. Make sure you let them come to room temperature before slicing and serving.

APPLE BOMBOLONI

Makes 9 or 10 doughnuts

In Italy, *bomboloni* are classic doughnuts, named after their bomblike shape. Whether in Trieste or Cividale, it's hard to visit any caffè for a morning espresso and not be tempted by these sweet treats waiting for you on the counter. The sweet yeasted egg-dough puffs up dramatically while cooking in hot oil, then the resulting orb is stuffed with a filling and powdered with sugar. What we like most about making them is getting the ratio of filling to doughnut just right (about 2 ounces of filling), be it lemon curd, fruit jam, or, my favorite in the fall, apple compote. This Friulano version contains eggs because it evolved from *Krapfen*, the Austrian variant of the Berliner; that's right, fried yeasted doughnuts exist in pretty much every country in the world! Try to keep your consumption to one per person, if you can.

Note

The flavor of the dough will be improved if you take the time to refrigerate it overnight (it will keep for up to 2 days), ahead of shaping and frying the doughnuts.

YOU WILL NEED

2-quart container

3½-inch cookie cutter

Deep-fryer (optional) or heavy pot with straight edges

Deep-frying thermometer

Piping bag fitted with medium-small plain tip

DOUGHNUT DOUGH

2¼ cups all-purpose flour	2 tablespoons crème fraîche
2 tablespoons granulated sugar	1 egg, plus 1 egg yolk
1 tablespoon active dry yeast (see Note, page 178)	1 teaspoon vanilla extract
¼ teaspoon kosher salt	½ cup whole milk
	2 tablespoons unsalted butter

APPLE COMPOTE

4 Honeycrisp apples, peeled, cored, and diced	½ cup packed dark brown sugar
¼ cup freshly squeezed orange juice	½ teaspoon freshly grated nutmeg
2 tablespoons freshly squeezed lemon juice	1 vanilla bean
	¼ teaspoon kosher salt

2 quarts canola oil	Confectioners' sugar for dusting

To make the dough: Generously butter a 2-quart container. In the bowl of a stand mixer fitted with the paddle attachment, combine the flour, granulated sugar, yeast, salt, crème fraîche, egg, egg yolk, and vanilla extract. Mix on medium-low speed until the mixture becomes sandy throughout, about 1 minute, then switch the paddle for the dough hook.

In a small saucepan over medium heat (or in a small bowl in the microwave), warm the milk and butter until the butter melts and the mixture feels warm to the touch (90° to 100°F). Pour into the mixer bowl.

Mix on medium-low speed for 10 minutes—the dough will look smooth long before then, but the long kneading is key. Stop the machine to scrape the bottom and sides of the bowl every so often to make sure everything is well incorporated. Transfer to the prepared container and cover tightly. Refrigerate until the dough doubles in size, at least 4 hours or up to overnight.

To make the compote: While the dough is proofing, in a medium saucepan over medium-high heat, combine the apples, orange juice, lemon juice, brown sugar, and nutmeg. Cut the vanilla bean lengthwise and scrape the seeds into the saucepan. Turn the heat to medium, cover, and simmer until the apples are tender and the juices have thickened into a thin syrup, about 15 minutes. Season with the salt. Transfer to a blender and puree until smooth, then set aside in the refrigerator.

Dust a work surface and a baking sheet with flour. Place the dough on the prepared surface and roll out to a ¼-inch-thick circle. Use a 3½-inch cookie cutter to cut out seven or so circles and transfer to the prepared baking sheet, keeping a space of 1 inch between each piece of dough. Gather the scraps of dough and kneed to a smooth ball before rolling again and cutting out two or three additional circles.

Let the dough proof on the baking sheet at room temperature for 1 hour; they will puff up slightly.

Toward the end of the proofing period, heat the canola oil in a deep fryer or a large pot to 335°F. Be sure to use a pot or Dutch oven with tall, straight edges and at least 3 inches of canola oil. Position a wire rack over a clean baking sheet.

Once the dough has proofed for 1 hour and the oil is at the correct temperature, add two or three dough circles to the oil. Be careful not to crowd the pot—cook them in batches. Fry on one side until golden, about 1 minute, then, using a wire skimmer, gently flip each doughnut over and fry until golden brown, another 1 to 1½ minutes. The doughnuts will puff up dramatically and increase to 4 to 5 inches in diameter. Transfer to the wire rack to cool. (Bomboloni, like all yeasted doughnuts, are best enjoyed the same day. These will keep for up to 8 hours at room temperature.)

Transfer the compote to a piping bag fitted with a medium-small plain tip. Using a small sharp knife, make a ½-inch incision on the side of each doughnut. Insert the tip of the bag into the incision and fill with about 2 tablespoons compote.

Dust the bombolini with confectioners' sugar before serving.

POPPY SEED AND CURRANT BISCOTTI

Makes about 20 biscotti

For this biscotti, we have taken a Friulano approach, combining white chocolate, orange, and poppy seeds (which, like many spices, were introduced to Friuli on their way from Trieste, a major spice port, to Vienna and Budapest). We don't like our biscotti to be super-crunchy and dry or, er, *rock* hard. Rather, there's an overall tenderness to these biscotti; they're a little chewy with white chocolate chunks and sweet currants.

¼ cup unsalted butter, at room temperature

¼ cup packed brown sugar

1 tablespoon granulated sugar

1 egg

⅔ cup all-purpose flour

¼ cup poppy seeds

½ teaspoon baking powder

Pinch of kosher salt

¼ cup chopped white chocolate

2 tablespoons currants

Finely grated zest of 1 orange

½ teaspoon vanilla extract

In a stand mixer fitted with the paddle attachment, on medium-high speed, cream the butter and both sugars until pale and well combined, about 3 minutes. Add the egg and keep mixing until combined, stopping the machine to scrape down the bowl as needed.

In a medium bowl, whisk together the flour, poppy seeds, baking powder, and salt.

With the mixer running on low speed, add the flour mixture to the butter mixture in three additions—it's okay if the flour is not completely incorporated. Add the chocolate, currants, orange zest, and vanilla and mix until all the ingredients are incorporated evenly, about 30 seconds. Refrigerate the dough (still in the mixer bowl) to rest for 1 hour.

Using your hands, gently shape the dough into an even 1½-inch-diameter log (to measure diameter, poke a cake tester or skewer through the log vertically, marking the point of entry with your finger, then measure the part of the tester that was in the log). Place the log on a plate and freeze for 20 minutes.

Preheat the oven to 325°F. Line a baking sheet with parchment paper.

Transfer the log onto the prepared baking sheet and bake for 30 minutes (the log will have spread out). Let the cookie log cool on the baking sheet for 25 to 30 minutes, then transfer, using a long spatula or chef's knife to support the log, to a cutting board. Using a serrated knife, cut the log on a slight diagonal angle into ½-inch-wide pieces (to get the shape of traditional biscotti).

Lay the slices cut-side down onto the prepared baking sheet and return to the oven to bake until golden brown around the edges, about 15 minutes. Let cool on the baking sheet. The biscotti will keep in an airtight container, at room temperature, for up to 1 week.

TORTA SABBIOSA MADELEINES

Makes 24 madeleines, or one 8-inch cake

This is the Frasca take on typical French madeleines (the little, shell-shaped, plump tea cakes). The batter used for these mini-cakes is that of a *Torta Sabbiosa*, a northern Italian specialty that means, quite literally, "sandy cake." Flavorwise, it is a cross between a pound cake and an angel food cake. The use of yeast (instead of a chemical leavener such as baking powder) imparts a distinctive, comforting aroma to this plain confection, both when it's baking and when you eat it. This is perfect with your first pull of espresso in the morning, or the last one after dinner.

Notes

Vanilla bean paste is especially nice in this recipe because the specks of vanilla pop against the plain cake crumb. Don't be tempted to replace it with vanilla bean seeds or extract. The madeleines won't be the same.

If you prefer, the batter can be baked as a whole cake in an 8-inch cake pan.

YOU WILL NEED

Instant-read digital thermometer
Two 12-cup madeleine pans or one 8-inch cake pan
Piping bag fitted with medium plain tip

⅓ cup water

1½ teaspoons active dry yeast

14 tablespoons unsalted butter, at room temperature

1 cup sugar

¼ teaspoon kosher salt

1 tablespoon vanilla bean paste (see Note)

2 eggs, at room temperature

1 cup all-purpose flour

¼ cup potato starch

Using a microwave, warm the water to approximately 104°F (but no hotter than 115°F); it should feel a little warmer than lukewarm. Stir in the yeast and set aside.

In a stand mixer fitted with the paddle attachment, combine the butter, sugar, salt, and vanilla bean paste. Beat at medium speed until creamy and light, about 3 minutes, stopping the machine as needed to scrape down the sides of the bowl with a spatula. Turn the speed to medium-low and add the eggs, one at a time, making sure the first is well combined before adding the next one, again stopping the mixer as needed to scrape down the sides. Pour in the yeast mixture and continue to mix on low speed until fully incorporated.

In a separate bowl, whisk together the flour and potato starch until just combined. With the mixer running on low speed, slowly add the flour–potato starch mixture, little by little, and mix until combined well.

Preheat the oven to 350°F. Butter and flour two madeleine pans or an 8-inch cake pan and place on a baking sheet.

Transfer the batter to a piping bag fitted with a medium plain tip, and pipe into each madeleine cavity, filling no more than three-fourths full. Let the batter sit at room temperature for 20 minutes, allowing the yeast to kick off its fermentation process.

Bake the madeleines until they are domed and their edges are golden brown, 18 to 20 minutes. If making the cake, bake for 45 minutes until golden brown and firm and a cake tester inserted in the center comes out clean.

Madeleines are best eaten day-of. The torta sabbiosa, however, will keep up in an airtight container, at room temperature, for up to 3 days.

STRAWBERRY TART

Makes one 10-inch tart; 8 servings

We know what you're thinking—an entire book on Italian cooking and culture, and then the last recipe is . . . French? Lachlan baked a lot of pastries in his Paris days; and at the French Laundry, we often had a beautiful tart on the menu. But it wasn't until strolling the streets of Trieste and the smaller mountain towns on early summer mornings that we saw such beautiful strawberry tarts. We serve this at Frasca on a *pasta frolla* (Italian shortcrust pastry) during peak strawberry season in Colorado. This dessert straddles the history of Lachlan's culinary journey, and we are so happy to share it!

YOU WILL NEED

Instant-read digital thermometer
10-inch tart pan with removable base
Dried beans, rice, or ceramic pie weights
Small offset spatula

PASTA FROLLA DOUGH

1 cup all-purpose flour, plus more for dusting	½ cup cold unsalted butter, cubed
¼ cup sugar	1 egg plus 1 egg yolk, beaten
⅛ teaspoon kosher salt	

SEMOLINA PASTRY CREAM

1½ cups whole milk	1 tablespoon unsalted butter
5 egg yolks	1 tablespoon orange blossom water
2 tablespoons sugar	
2 tablespoons plus 1 teaspoon semolina flour	Finely grated zest of 1 orange

MACERATED STRAWBERRIES

4 cups vertically sliced strawberries	½ cup sugar

To make the dough: In the bowl of a food processor fitted with the dough blade, combine the flour, sugar, salt, and butter and pulse until well blended, four to five pulses, or blend the ingredients together in a large bowl with a fork or pastry blender, until the butter is the size of small peas.

Add the beaten egg to the food processor (or to the bowl if you are making this by hand) and process, five to seven pulses, or blend until a rough-looking dough starts to form. Gather the dough into a disk, wrap in plastic, and refrigerate it for at least 1 hour or up to overnight (take the dough out 15 minutes before rolling to soften slightly).

To make the pastry cream: Meanwhile, fill a large bowl with ice cubes and cold water to form an ice bath and then set a medium bowl on top.

In a small saucepan over medium heat, bring the milk to scalding. In a medium bowl, whisk the egg yolks, sugar, and semolina flour until very well combined, about 2 minutes.

Pour ¼ cup of the hot milk into the yolk mixture and whisk well. Return the tempered mixture to the saucepan, turn the heat to medium-low, and cook, stirring continuously, until it registers 180° to 182°F on a thermometer.

Transfer the mixture to the bowl set over the ice bath; add the butter, orange blossom water, and orange zest; and then whisk until well combined. Place plastic wrap of the surface of the mixture and set aside in the refrigerator.

Preheat the oven to 350°F. Lightly butter a 10-inch tart pan.

Flatten the dough with a rolling pin, then roll between two sheets of parchment paper into a 12- to 13-inch circle. Remove the top piece of paper. Dust the top of the dough lightly with flour, then fold it in fourths. Lift the dough and place it with the point of the fold in the center of the prepared tart pan. Gently unfold the dough and fit it into the pan, allowing any excess to drape over the sides. Trim the edges with scissors and press the dough manually to make it

continued

even with the top of the pan. Poke the dough all over with a fork. Place a sheet of aluminum foil over the top of the dough and weigh it down with dried beans, rice, or ceramic pie weights; this will help prevent the tart shell from puffing up as it bakes. Set the tart mold on a baking sheet.

Bake the tart shell for 10 minutes, then remove the foil and beans and bake until it is golden around the edges and cooked through (the base should look dry), about 10 minutes longer. Transfer the tart shell to a wire rack to cool.

To prepare the strawberries: In a medium bowl, gently combine the strawberries and sugar. Set aside to macerate, allowing the strawberries to release their juices, 30 minutes or so, and then drain.

Spoon the pastry cream into the tart shell and use an offset spatula to spread the cream and smooth the surface. Arrange the strawberries in an overlapping spiral, starting on the outside and working your way into the center. Serve immediately.

OUR FRIULI ADDRESS BOOK

When on your way to Friuli, if you're arriving or departing through Venice, we highly recommend beginning (or ending) your trip at Osteria Alle Testiere, our favorite Venetian restaurant. It is the only address outside of Friuli Venezia Giulia on the following list.

Land

Allegria hotel
Vicolo Chiuso, 1, 33100 Udine UD, Italy

Astoria Hotel Italia
Piazza XX Settembre, 24, 33100 Udine UD, Italy

Bar Rullo
Piazza XXIV Maggio, 27, Cormons GO, Italy

D'Osvaldo Prosciutti
Via Dante, 40, 34071 Cormons GO, Italy

Enoteca di Cormons
Piazza XXIV Maggio, 21, 34071 Cormons GO, Italy

Fattoria Zoff Agriturismo Borg da Ocjs dairy farm
Via Parini, 18, 34071 Cormons GO, Italy

La Frasca restaurant
Viale Grado, 50, 33050 Lauzacco UD, Italy

L'Argine a Vencò restaurant
Località Vencò, 34070 Dolegna del Collio GO, Italy

La Subida Country Resort—Trattoria al Cacciatore
Via Subida, 52, 34071 Cormons GO, Italy

Molino Tuzzi mill
Località Trussio Ruttars, 5, 34070 Dolegna del Collio GO, Italy

Osteria Al Cappello
Via Paolo Sarpi, 5, 33100 Udine UD, Italy

Osteria Al Vecchio Stallo
Via Viola 7, 33100 Udine UD, Italy

Ristorante Agli Amici
Via Liguria, 252, 33100 Udine UD, Italy

Ristorante Campiello
Via Nazionale, 40, 33048 San Giovanni Al Natisone UD, Italy

Ristorante La Primula
Via S. Rocco, 47, 33080 San Quirino PN, Italy

Ristorante Le Dune
Via Dante, 41, 34070 Mariano del Friuli GO, Italy

Ristorante Vitello d'Oro
Via Erasmo Valvason, 4, 33100 Udine UD, Italy

Trattoria Al Grop
Via G. Matteotti, 7, 33010 Tavagnacco UD, Italy

Trattoria Al Parco
Via Stretta, 7, 33042 Buttrio UD, Italy

Trattoria Toso
Via Pozzuolo, 16, 33019 Leonacco UD, Italy

Sea

Caffè San Marco
Via Cesare Battisti, 18, 34125 Trieste TS, Italy

Cremcaffè
Piazza Carlo Goldoni, 10, 34122 Trieste TS, Italy

Harry's Piccolo Restaurant & Bistrò
Piazza Unità d'Italia, 2, 34121 Trieste TS, Italy

Lokanda Devetak
San Michele del Carso, Via Brežiči, 22, 34070 Savogna d'Isonzo GO, Italy

Masè Cured Meats
Via J. Ressel, 2, 34018 San Dorligo della Valle TS, Italy

Osteria Alle Testiere
Calle del Mondo Novo, 5801, 30122 Venezia VE, Italy

Ristorante Ai Fiori
Piazza Attilio Hortis, 7, 34124 Trieste TS, Italy

Ristorante Al Bagatto
Via Luigi Cadorna, 7, 34124 Trieste TS, Italy

Stella Polare café
Via Dante Alighieri, 14, 34121 Trieste TS, Italy

Tavernetta All'Androna
Calle Porta Piccola, 6, 34073 Grado GO, Italy

Trattoria Ai Ciodi
34073 Grado GO, Italy

Trattoria Da Giovanni
Via S. Lazzaro, 14, 34122 Trieste TS, Italy

Mountains

Agriturismo La Planina
Via Plagnava, Case Specognal 1, 33040 Castelmonte UD, Italy

Albergo Neider
Sauris di Sopra, 38, 33020 Sauris di Sotto UD, Italy

Caffé Moderno
Via Caduti II Maggio, 155, 33025 Ovaro UD, Italy

Farm Malga Montasio
33010 Sella Nevea, Chiusaforte UD, Italy

La Casa del Prosciutto "Alberti 1906"
Via Teobaldo Ciconi, 24, 33038 San Daniele del Friuli UD, Italy

Locanda Da Dino restaurant
Via Patuscera di Entrampo, 20, 33025 Ovaro UD, Italy

Matoga Café Di Topan Stefano
Via Ex Ferrovia, 31, 33025 Ovaro UD, Italy

Michele Massaro (iron worker and knifemaker)
Antica Forgia Lenarduzzi di Michele Massaro
Via Tesana Nord, 75, 33085 Maniago PN, Italy

Osteria Al Portonat
Piazza Dante Alighieri, 7, 33038 San Daniele del Friuli UD, Italy

Osteria Da Alvise
Via I Maggio, 5, 33020 Sutrio UD, Italy

Osteria Pizzeria Allo Zoncolan
Piazza Panto' di 5, Via Liariis, 33025 Ovaro UD, Italy

Prosciuttificio Wolf Sauris
Sauris di Sotto, 88, 33020 Sauris di Sotto UD, Italy

Ristorante Alla Pace
Via Sauris di Sotto 38, 33020 Sauris di Sotto UD, Italy

Ristorante Laite
Borgata Hoffe, 10, 32012 Sappada UD, Italy

ACKNOWLEDGMENTS

This book would not of have come into place without so many people nudging us in the right direction. First, thank you to Meredith Erickson for working with us for almost three years on this project. You captured our spirit in this book and elevated it! To Peter Hoglund, our partner, for all his encouragement and helping us stay the course. To Alicia York, Erin Pommer, Rose Votta, and the entire Frasca team for helping us stay focused on this long journey while diligently keeping a close eye on Frasca when we were away. To Chefs Kelly Jeun, Eduardo Valle Lobo, and Alberto Hernandez for their inspiration and contribution to the book on so many levels. To William Hereford for spending all the time with us on the photography of this book, early in the morning and late into the evening, you were a dream to work with. To the region of Friuli and its amazing producers, chefs, and hospitalians that have welcomed the Frasca Family and our guests into their special world. There are literally hundreds of people to thank in person; but Christian Patat and Serena Palazzolo most of all—thanks for all your support of us, our passion, and dreams!

To Mitja, Tanja, Loredana, Jŏsko, and Sandro for the warmth and always a bed to sleep in. Ever since our first visit in 2003, we have been forever changed by La Subida. To Andrea Felluga for all the historical advice and a lot of smiles. Last, and maybe most critical to it all, to Ten Speed Press for thinking it was perfectly normal for a restaurant in Boulder, Colorado, to write a book on an Italian region called Friuli.

We hope you all enjoy the book.

Bobby would like to thank: Danette Stuckey for believing in me when I said I wanted to leave Napa Valley and the cocoon of the French Laundry to open a restaurant inspired by the region of Friuli Venezia Giulia. To the amazing guests of Boulder and beyond who have decided to be on the journey with us. To my mom, Linda Stuckey, for thinking it was okay for me to be a busboy. To my father, Larry Stuckey, who really thought it was better to be a server than an insurance sales associate (my father owned an insurance company).

Lachlan would like to thank: First, my mom and dad (Susan and Alec) for always believing in me despite having no idea how this journey would unfold. As two successful surgeons, I can only now imagine the anxiety you both must have felt when I passed on grad school and decided to move to Paris to explore my dream of being a chef. While it wasn't a path you knew, and likely freaked you out, all I felt was the support that I could succeed. The work ethic and drive you instilled in me as I was growing up allowed me to overcome every challenge I faced then and to this day. To my darling wife, Cristin, who saved me when I needed it most and to this day, and every day, adores us and our life together. Thank you for giving me the ability to keep charging forward. To my children, Lydia, Julian, and Calvin; you have taught me what life and love are all about. Looking forward to seeing you all live out your dreams. It is hard to imagine where I would be without the love and support of my family.

Meredith would like to thank: Bobby and Lachlan for introducing me to the magic that is FVG. I'm forever transformed and grateful. Thank you to the Sirk family for opening the doors of La Subida and for opening my eyes to the incredible surrounding culture. Thank you to William for your photos and ability to make us all laugh, all the time. Thank you to my partner in recipe-testing-and-developing crime, Kendra McKnight. To our editors, Julie Bennett and Doug Ogan, thank you. And to the Ten Speed Press design and production teams, Kara Plikaitis, Kelly Booth, and Jane Chinn, thank you.

INDEX

All rights reserved.
Published in the United States by Ten Speed Press,
an imprint of Random House, a division of Penguin
Random House LLC, New York.
www.tenspeed.com

Ten Speed Press and the Ten Speed Press colophon are
registered trademarks of Penguin Random House LLC.

Library of Congress Cataloging-in-Publication Data
is on file with the publisher.

Hardcover ISBN: 978-0-399-58061-1
eBook ISBN: 978-0-399-58062-8

Printed in China

Design by Kara Plikaitis
Page 12: Friuli Venezia Giulia map by
   Tim McGinty with Karen Clark

10 9 8 7 6 5 4 3 2 1

First Edition